The Third Age of
Broadcasting

The Third Age of Broadcasting

Edited by Brian Wenham

Paul Bonner, Melvyn Bragg,
Russell Harty, Stephen Hearst,
Peter Ibbotson, Robert MacNeil,
David Puttnam, Robert Rowland,
Brian Wenham

faber and faber

First published in 1982
by Faber and Faber Limited
3 Queen Square London WC1N 3AU
Printed in Great Britain by
Redwood Burn Ltd Trowbridge Wiltshire

© Paul Bonner, Melvyn Bragg, Russell Harty,
Stephen Hearst, Peter Ibbotson, Robert MacNeil,
David Puttnam, Robert Rowland, Brian Wenham, 1982

British Library Cataloguing in Publication Data

The Third age of broadcasting
1. Television broadcasting
I. Wenham, Brian
384.55'4   HE8700.4
ISBN 0–571–11981–6

I can only wonder at the great distances we have come since, in 1936, I watched at Alexandra Palace the first television programme being transmitted and be glad that in Britain the great and ancient institution of Parliament is still linked with the strange new medium of television and that each in its own way has endeavoured to promote throughout the world the freedom of the individual.

Thankfulness, however, is not enough. Hope is also necessary: hope that the qualities of British broadcasting will be able to survive and be developed in a world of dizzyingly rapid technical, social and political change.

Grace Wyndham Goldie
Facing the Nation: Television and Politics, 1936–76

Contents

About the Contributors

PAUL BONNER   Born Surrey, 1934. After two years in publishing and journalism, joined the BBC in Bristol in 1955 and moved to the London Television Talks Department in 1960. Started *Choice*, the first television consumer programme. As documentary producer, made *Search for the Real Che Guevara*, and *Who Sank the* Lusitania. Editor of BBC Community Programmes 1974; head of BBC Television Science and Features 1978; joined Channel Four as Channel Controller in October 1980.

MELVYN BRAGG   Born Wigton, Cumberland, 1939. Took a degree in Modern History at Oxford. His novels include *For Want of a Nail*, *The Hired Man*, *Josh Lawton*, *Autumn Manoeuvres*, and *Kingdom Come*. Has also written 'Speak for England', an oral history of England since 1900. His television career began in the BBC, on 'Monitor'. He is now head of the Arts Department at London Weekend Television and editor and presenter of the 'South Bank Show'. His screenwriting credits include *Isadora*, *The Music Lovers* and *Jesus Christ Superstar*.

RUSSELL HARTY   Born Blackburn, Lancashire, 1934. Took a degree in English at Oxford. For eleven years a teacher in Giggleswick and in New York City. Producer BBC Radio 3 1968 to 1970. Worked on London Weekend's *Aquarius* from 1970 to 1973 and since then has stepped in front of the camera in diverse entertainments, both for ITV and for the BBC. From time to time columnist for newspapers and periodicals.

STEPHEN HEARST   Born Vienna, 1919. Joined BBC TV as a newsreel scriptwriter in 1952. In 1965 became executive producer of arts programmes and, in 1967, head of Arts Features. Series under his aegis included *Civilization* with Kenneth Clark, and Alistair Cooke's *America*. In 1972 became Controller of Radio 3 and in 1978 moved to the post of Controller Future Policy, in effect head of the

11

BBC's Think Tank. Publications include *2,000 Million Poor* and *Artistic Heritage and its Treatment by Television*.

PETER IBBOTSON   Born Salford, 1943. Took a degree in Modern History at Oxford. Abandoned brief academic career in 1967 for bright lights of television. Worked for London Weekend and for Thames Television before moving to the BBC in 1971. Producer on *Panorama, Tonight* and *Newsday*. Since 1979 editor of the *Newsweek* on BBC-2.

ROBERT MACNEIL   Born Canada, 1931. Has worked in television extensively in Britain and in the United States—three months at ITN, five years at NBC, eight years at the BBC, mostly with *Panorama*. Since 1975 has worked for the Public Broadcasting System in the United States, as editor and co-presenter of the nightly *MacNeil–Lehrer Report*. Author of *The People Machine* and—just published in the USA—*The Right Place at the Right Time*.

DAVID PUTTNAM   Born London, 1941. After a career in advertising, moved into film production in late 1960s. Followed *Melody* with *Pied Piper, That'll Be the Day, Mahler, Lisztomania, Stardust, Bugsy Malone, The Duelists, Midnight Express, Foxes* and, in 1981, *Chariots of Fire*, which received four Oscars and numerous other international awards. Currently producing for the cinema *Local Hero*, starring Burt Lancaster and directed by Bill Forsyth, and for Channel Four television a series of films under the title *First Love*.

ROBERT ROWLAND   Born Chesterfield, 1937. President of the Union at Oxford, where he took a degree in Modern History. Joined BBC as a general trainee in 1961 and worked as film director on *Panorama*, becoming deputy editor in 1967. Thereafter deputy editor *Nationwide* (1969); editor *Money Programme* (1970); editor *Panorama* (1972). In 1973 he took over as Head of the BBC's Open University Department. Closely involved in the planning and building of Europe's largest purpose-built educational production centre at Milton Keynes, which opened in September 1981.

BRIAN WENHAM   Born London, 1937. Took a degree in Modern History at Oxford. Worked for Independent Television News from 1962 to 1969. Moved to BBC in 1969 as editor of *Panorama*. Became Head of BBC Current Affairs in 1971 and Controller of BBC-2 in 1978.

Foreword: So as to Choose

"I shall always tell you whenever I see you taking what seems to me too much liberty."

"Pray do; but I don't say I shall always think your remonstrance just."

"Very likely not. You're too fond of your own ways."

"Yes, I think I'm very fond of them. But I always want to know the things one shouldn't do."

"So as to do them?" asked her aunt.

"So as to choose," said Isabel.

Henry James
Portrait of a Lady

Britain is on the brink of a Third Age of Broadcasting, in which the expansion of the means of distribution will permit an explosion of television programming beyond the wildest dreams of early pioneers.

So far public debate about how to proceed has been virtually non-existent; parliamentary debate is as yet perfunctory and unformed; professional debate is partly pushed forward by the search for easy profits, partly held back by institutional paranoia at what pro-liferation might bring.

The contributors to this volume differ sharply in their willingness to embrace the future both in general and in terms of the particular enticements held out in the areas they know best, but in one matter they are agreed.

What we can do tells us little about what we should do. Much is technologically possible, but nothing need be determined by technology alone. What use Britain makes of new broadcast opportunities should reflect the rub of other pressures—political, commercial, sociological and moral too. These pressures and their wider implications and motivations should be subjected to the closest scrutiny. In other words, we need nothing less than a full and open debate, from which no viewer should feel debarred.

It is, then, in this spirit that these essays are offered, not as definitive statements but as initial probes into tomorrow's broadcasting interior. They are designed to mark out new paths for further examination and inquiry so as—at the end of the day—the better to choose.

B.W.

13

1. Into the Interior

BRIAN WENHAM

The first two ages of British broadcasting each lasted about thirty years. The first age, that of radio domination, began in 1922 and ended in 1953, when the pageantry of the Coronation triggered a transfer of power and of popularity from radio to the infant television. The second age, from 1953 to today, has been the Golden Age of Rationed Television. BBC-1, then ITV, then BBC-2 have been fashioned into a programme service of flexibility and of force, deliberately but delicately regulated by the BBC and the IBA in accordance with the wishes of the Parliaments of the time. But now, just around the corner, lie the twin developments of increased picture transmission by satellite and by cable. Just how, and how quickly, they will be allowed and encouraged to develop is a matter for open speculation, but there can be no doubt that the end of rationing that they imply will administer drastic shocks to the traditional mechanisms of broadcast production, distribution and exchange and to the regulatory arrangements that have sustained them.

The start of Channel Four is at one and the same time the final chapter in the old story and the first paragraph in the new. No fresh form of distribution will be involved; indeed, the fourth button has been present but unpushed for years. Furthermore, the Channel is under the familiar auspices of the IBA, with the equally familiar jingle of advertisements ringing up the cash, so not much new there. But in the particulars of production Channel Four marks a significant departure, in that for the first time a television channel will carry a substantial amount of independent work. Hitherto virtually all television production has been in-house, in the hands of the staffs of the BBC and of the ITV companies. Notions about what consitutes a good, professional programme have become common to both sides of the industry, as have the general codes concerning balance in matters of political and public interest and restraint in matters of language, violence and explicit indicators of sexual exuberance. Inevitably, an independent sector, largely peopled by refugees from the alleged artistic brutalities of existing regimes, will seek to challenge those codes and the assumptions behind them. For the moment the IBA brandishes the existing rule book, as it must, and asserts that new, independent programming must in all essentials toe the line; but non-house-trained producers will be tempted, perhaps expected, to overstep it out of ignorance, mischief or simply a sense of fun. And we shall begin, perhaps, to see something of where the alternative broadcasting of the future could lead.

But well before the ink on the charter of Channel Four television is properly dry, we shall be hard up against Channels Five and Six. They have already been given the go-ahead by the Home Secretary, in his early 1982 announcement about satellite broadcasting. Beyond them stand Channels Seven, Eight and Nine, to complete Britain's entitlement to broadcast on up to five satellite channels. And alongside, taking advantage this time not of satellite but of cable, sits the prospect of a further ten, twenty, thirty channels, or even more, in those areas of the country that chance to be wired up. But to take advantage of these heady developments, the viewer will first have to get himself properly geared up, and that may well expose him to a line of charges greatly in excess of today's.

At the moment the householder is at risk for some £3 per week. He has to equip himself with a set and an aerial, but the highly developed rental market can keep the weekly cost of these to around £2. On top of that he must pay the basic licence of under £1 per week to see three, and soon four, channels in colour, or, if he prefers to linger in black-and-white, he can get the same programming for a weekly cost of 29p. Tomorrow's new programming will not come as cheaply. Sets will need to be adjusted both for additional channel capacity and for decoders that distinguish who gets a particular service and who does not. No hard estimates yet exist and the rental industry will doubtless strive to make the weekly mark-up as small as possible, but mark-up there will be. Then for satellite reception the viewer will require a dish or possibly, in time, a panel on an outside wall. Estimates for these currently run in the £250–£350 range, although mass marketing may make a large dent in that. Those sufficiently advantaged to be wired into a cable system may side-step this satellite hardware charge, but they will face instead a basic cable charge for the delivery

16

of the multi-channel system. That charge is unlikely to be below £100 a year. And, of course, on top of the various charges for equipment and distribution will come charges for the new forms of programming themselves: say, £100 to be plugged into a special form of local sports service; say, a fiver just to watch a Big Fight in the privacy of your own home. The technology exists to permit all these variations in pricing. Indeed, at the end of the line lies the know-how for a full-blooded system of pay-per-view, under which each act of viewing would be metered and charged out, much as we are charged for the use of electricity, gas or the telephone.

Faced with such a Hydra-headed set of challenges to the simplicities of today's broadcasting economics, many conventional broadcasters would rather that the whole expansionist future went away. Many viewers may come to echo that wish. Why not pull up the drawbridge after Channel Four gets through? Why not settle for fleshing out the four channels, building on the breakfast television that is to come, on through the mornings and, eventually, into the early hours as well? Too bad if the Department of Industry bemoans the loss of industrial opportunity. Britain, it is widely said, has the best broadcasting in the world. Why let rash development and deregulation ruin it?

At this point in the argument we must confront the video recorder. One of the major commercial surprises of recent years has been the rapid spread of domestic recorders in a period of deep recession. By the end of 1982 it is estimated that one home in ten will have equipped itself with what is essentially a protest against the limitations of rationed television. The protest is in part violent and pornographic, in that the appetite for super-X films is not met by broadcast television but can be met by the video corner-store. But a much larger part of the protest would seem to be connected with the frustration of scheduling conventions that oblige *you* to watch programmes at times decided by people like *me*. And behind that desire for each man to be his own scheduler lies the assertion that choice must ultimately be viewer-based, not broadcaster-determined. Many viewers seem prepared to back this assertion with hard cash and, in so doing, reveal that whatever the moans about the level of the licence fee, they are in practice content to divert more and more of their leisure budget to the television set and the messages coming out of it. That is the marketing truth at the heart of the third age.

So it is no use standing pat, like some First World War general, muttering 'Ils ne passeront pas.' The citadel is surrounded, and the walls are already being chipped away. The valid debate now concerns what sorts of special claim traditional broadcasting should make against incursions by the newcomers. And here consideration must be given not just to what the new technology can do but also to what it cannot. Both satellite and cable are divisive. With satellite the division is economic: in theory all could receive it, but in practice many would find it hard to afford the combined costs of the hardware and the service. Cable is divisive both economically and socially. Even the most enthusiastic proponent of cable admits that the prime target is the half of the country that lives in built-up areas. There is no guarantee that cable, with its ultimate prize of moving from channels in single figures to channels in the forties and fifties, will ever be available to all. In other words, we are dealing with an additional facility for some, not with a utility for all.

This central characteristic of the new technology gives us a clue as to how we might proceed. In a nutshell, the claim of the basic citizen-viewer must be that until such time as new technologies are available at par to all, expansion of service should be arranged and guided so as not to deprive the viewer-of-networks of what he or she now receives. That means, in the first place, that the viewer-by-cable should automatically receive the basic networks as part of his or her cable package; in the second place, and more critically, it means that the non-cable and non-satellite viewer should continue to receive a programme mix of which the standard, quality and variety are similar to those presently enjoyed. The difficulty here, of course, is that it may well be that the easiest way forward for the *new*, third age television services will be to plunder the proven attractions of the *old*. Thus we arrive at the nub of the problem and the central equation in terms of which would-be expansionists should be judged.

The BBC proposals for the first two satellite channels, Channel Five and Channel Six, take care to propose services that are genuine additions to what is already on offer. The Channel Five proposition is to offer by satellite a service comprising mainly newly released feature films, but to offer it much earlier than would normally be available to the basic network viewer. Current practice imposes an interval of at least three years between the cinema première of a film and its subsequent release on network television. American experience indicates that this gap is also a launch window, bringing the box office, in effect, direct into the home, in return for a fee. In theory, the cinema distributor would be the loser, but in Britain cinema distribution has long since lost. Attendances are already down to 6 per cent of 1947 levels. The new service, therefore, recognizes what has long been a truth—most Britons prefer to see films on television rather than in cinemas. The hard bargaining will be concerned with how the proceeds of such an operation should be recycled into more and better films, not used to prop up a bypassed display system. American experience, coupled with the evidence from pioneer British cable exercises, makes it reasonable to assume that 1 million or more subscribers would want to avail themselves of a satellite domestic box office. At £100 per annum per viewer, such an operation would yield the budget of BBC-2, even slightly more.

The proposals for Channel Six, again a BBC satellite channel, are less well defined. Behind the banner 'Window on the World', the BBC is examining a mix of programming that would incorporate the best of international television, some sustaining service of international news and the pick of British programming, past and present. This last aspect has elicited an obvious sneer: if the new service is to be based in part on repeats, what price the already repeat-laden BBC-1 and BBC-2? The sneer reflects the fact that 'repeat' is still a dirty word in television. It should not be. Indeed, one of the odder characteristics of broadcast television is that it assumes, quite erroneously, that a single transmission of most programmes will somehow ensure that the programme reaches the best part of its target audience. No other medium of information or entertainment operates in this way. Theatres and cinemas thrive on long runs; newspapers and periodicals exploit the ability to return, in editorials or in letters, day after day, week after week, to the same theme; books you can hold in your hand and keep. But television customarily spends itself with the utmost profligacy. A moment's thought indicates how bizarre the practice is. With three channels, my chance of missing any transmission is two out of three; with four channels, the chance increases to three out of four. Quite clearly, good television programmes, like films, should be able to come round the circuit time and again, more and more cobwebbed, perhaps, but still showing some signs of life. Any viewer could name you ten things he or she would love to see again. The aggregates of those desires could form the underpinning of at least one channel, if not more.

Present plans call for the 'Window on the World' to be financed by a small supplementary licence levied on all those who opt for satellite transmission as an extra. Whether such a service could alternatively pay its own way by subscription or by advertising cannot and probably will never be known. It is, however, encouraging that the notion of a general fee unrelated to specific use still breathes, because the likeliest and best use for Channel Seven is one which would almost certainly have to be carried on a central vote. I refer, of course, to the televising of the proceedings of Parliament. The long Falkland spring and summer of 1982, which saw Britain grope towards a fresh understanding of her power, her conscience and her will, has graphically reminded us of where the centre of this democracy lies. It now verges on the outrageous that the viewer cannot be present at Parliament's deliberations but must wait instead for the practised but second-hand ministrations of Robin Day, Brian Walden and the rest. Increasingly, MPs are coming to share in this frustration, or so I sense. In the past the stumbling-block has always been Parliament's reluctance to offer free editing rights to undertakings as frisky (and possibly frivolous) as television. But the increase in channels now means that on one channel Parliament could be broadcast in full, enabling television to be as much a medium of record as Hansard is. True there would still need to be some minor demarcation machinery as between Commons and Lords, as between the Whole House and Committee, but for practical purposes a full account could now be broadcast. Editing and excerpting would continue on all networks, but in the knowledge that it would have to be seen to be justified in the light of the full service available elsewhere.

In looking for contenders for Channel Eight, both logic and economics oblige us to look abroad. The broadcasting revolution is not confined to Britain. International arrangements allow all countries to take up an allocation of five channels for satellite broadcasting. These channels are by no means as tidy or as controllable as conventional terrestrial transmission. The footprints of the station signals spill over far beyond the boundaries of each target country. In other words, international television is on the way to becoming as freely available as international radio. True, you would need constantly to update and realign your dish aerial and your receiver, and no doubt only the keenest boffins would test availability to the full, but for all of us the essential broadcasting truth is that we are no longer a television island.

Opinions vary as to what this will mean in practice. The best guess is that the traffic out will be far larger than the traffic in. Already in Holland and Belgium cable companies pirate British programming and distribute it to an interested public; the Republic of Ireland has had access to British television for years, although only within the Pale. I find it difficult to envisage much reverse flow. Perhaps I am simply too much of a Little Englander to take keen interest in what France, Germany or Italy may have to offer. I ignore their radio and have done so all my life.

A development that would engage me, however, would be one designed specifically to play to Europe's strength as a centre for the high arts of opera, orchestral and instrumental music and classical dance and drama. Suppose the major orchestras, opera houses and national theatres of Europe came together to provide for subscribers between thirty and forty hours a week of the best of what they do. Language would be no major problem, in that devotees would be used to tackling the works in original languages. Indeed, television has a particular advantage, in that the subtitle can be of positive assistance. My enjoyment of the Beyreuth *Parsifal* broadcast on Good Friday of 1982 outdistanced my enjoyment of earlier *Parsifals* precisely because I knew in detail what was being said. I believe I would be willing to undertake subtitled Racine on television; I am less sure that I would have the nerve to tackle him in French in the theatre. Furthermore, the queues at the doors of Europe's opera houses, taken with the price of the tickets, leads me to suppose that an enterprising consortium might find a ready and willing market of, say 2 million subscribers across Western Europe, each happy to offer up a minimum of £100 for this particular set of armchair pleasures. Even allowing for overheads, £200 million spread over 365 days seems an attractive enough working budget. It may be far-fetched to assume that a Europe that has brought us *Jeux sans frontières* and the *Eurovision Song Contest* could rise to such a challenge, but the economics seem very enticing and convincing enough to warrant a marker put down for Channel Eight.

For a ninth generally available channel, I would, with reluctance, return to the Falklands crisis and what that seemed to be saying about television news, with or without current affairs. Those of us who have spent part of our working lives in broadcast news know that it tends to expand to fill the time available. It aspires to the status of an industry. It became a day-long industry first on American radio, then

21

on British radio, then more recently on American television, and it would be a bold commentator who assumed that British television would lag too far behind. However, it may well be that there is insufficient will in post-imperial and relatively impoverished Britain to sustain the international reach of American models. A greater motivation may emerge from the floor up, from cable systems desperate for some basic interconnection that would both keep them going when all else failed and also provide an element that could be paraded as distinct. In other words, the push for a national and international all-news operation might come not from satellite Channel Nine, but from cable companies looking for a lynch-pin. Whether it was worth anyone's while putting such a service on satellite as well would then be a secondary consideration.

What else can be said of cable? What are its particular attractions likely to be to those areas lucky enough, or vulnerable enough, to get it? In the first place, I take it as axiomatic that any cable operation worth its salt will seek to carry as part of its basic provision not only the four terrestrial channels but the full allocation of five satellite channels as well. After all, the chief charm of cable to the potential subscriber is that it provides easy access to what otherwise might be cumbersome to come by. However, although these basic services may well keep cable companies ticking over, they are unlikely to make them rich. And most cable companies do sincerely want to be rich.

You might well suppose that in the long term riches, or at least a healthy living, will come locally. Companies will be locally sustained by fulfilling local needs. There is no long-term reason why local cable should not take on the mantle of the local press and the local radio and make it glow far more brightly. This is the area where even the best motivated network television leaves huge gaps. Both sides of the existing duopoly labour under the central difficulty that the areas designated for their local coverage are simply far too large.

Note, too, that much of the superstructure of cable in its second phase will come from data services rather than programming, and the thrust of these too will be locally based. In prospect are a whole range of information exchanges designed to change the way in which we shop, bank, work and sell. Many of these proposed refinements may seem frivolous or unnecessary in mid-recession. There are also some who argue that the job can be done well enough by the telephone, suitably adjusted to offer printed material. But these arguments lack conviction. The telephone has its work cut out simply being a telephone. Better, surely, to let local cable show what it can do.

Yet the debate about cable is not conducted in these relaxed, local terms. We are told that cable will flourish only if it develops major entertainments and attractions of its own, over and above the entertainments and attractions relayed by existing services. Why such little confidence in the plainer fare that would seem so ideally suited to local needs and therefore to cable systems? Part of the answer lies in the way Britain has chosen to stumble into cable. Having ignored the technology for a generation, converts and enthusiasts are now pressing for quick entry, and they expect private enterprise to bear the entire burden. Hence the requirement for a quick return, a quick kill. The current estimate of £2,500 million to cable the urban half of Britain is, if accurate, not necessarily a tall order if you take the long, or even the medium, view. It works out, after all, at around £250 for each of 10 million homes. At that level of investment, is it too late to consider public monies taking a stake in cable, the better perhaps to check any untoward capitalist overheating?

Certainly, in the United States local and public authorities make a point of having a large say in how cable operates, even when they leave the ownership to private enterprise. Much of the civic good exists in the promise rather than in the performance, but contract after contract spells out the need for local access for those wishing to broadcast simple programming, and for proper provision for the purveyance of local information, and for programming of relevance to the educationalists and to the arts. Admittedly, all this high-mindedness can be carried too far. There is, somewhere along the line, a *reductio ad absurdum* in access broadcasting. If your dog fouls my footpath, then better I tell you to your face. No need to make a television programme about the most minor of grievances simply because the technology exists that allows me to do so.

In the end, though, pondering the poverty of the cable debate in Britain, one is forced to a further and obvious conclusion. The imprecisions about what cable might have to offer are not sinister. The plain fact is that the would-be cable operators have not yet thought it through. And there is quite a lot to think through. It has taken thirty years for the combined weight of both the BBC and ITV to fill the screens with a mere three choices. There is already evident nervousness about the sturdiness of the programming to be offered by the fourth. Small wonder that the imagination boggles and turns in on itself at the blank sheets of paper presented by twenty, thirty or forty more. And to find any kind of decent answers you almost certainly have to forsake the broad-brush approach of four-channel network television—and forsake, too, the overall targeting implied by the suggestions for Britain's five satellite channels—and look for local needs and enthusiasms that will be as many and various as are the inhabitants of these islands.

Thus, for example, taking advantage of satellite overspill, a cable operation in Bedford, which has a substantial Italian population, might warm to the sight of Italian programming, pulled down from the satellite especially for them. Immigrant pockets in other areas might be similarly served or might serve themselves. No network will ever devote to the black or to the Asian viewers the close attention to their tastes and interests that could be provided by cable. And it is a mistake to assume that such services could never be afforded. Go today to the right video stores in areas of Indian and Pakistani settlement and you will find a growing trade in special programming and special films, precisely because the appetite for these is largely ignored by networks. Nor does the potential stop at ethnic or religious minorities. A colleague who had spent time in the United States examining the wild explosion of cable in that country came to the conclusion that you had to realize that what in this country is the occasional half-hour programme, say once or twice a week, can under cable conditions become a full-time, day-long, seven-days-a-week undertaking. Hence channels for women's programmes, channels for religion in many guises and so on.

Perhaps, however, nothing better illustrates what might be done, and the fights and conflicts that could arise, than the whole confused and contrary world of sport. Here we see all too plainly the outlines of a battle royal between the general viewer of networks and his interests and the selected viewer of cable and his aspirations. Undoubtedly, once cable had begun to dig in and consolidate, a large number of the fans of a particular sport would stump up to see the Test Matches, the Cup Final, the Open Golf, on a pay-per-view basis, if that was the only way they could get armchair access to them. Equally certainly, such arrangements would be a major strike against the democratic universality of provision that has so far characterized our handling of the top events in British sport.

But in the hinterland beyond the big occasion a slightly different picture begins to emerge. Despite what you may already think about the apparent overcrowding of the screens with sport, the plain fact is that what we see is but a fraction of what we could see. Most sport on television is tightly edited. There is more, much more, where the highlights came from. And there are loyal followings of 1 million and upwards for a whole range of sports that, from the point of view of the true fan, get scant coverage from television. Add, too, the uncomfortable fact that most sport is played at the weekend, when the clash of sport with sport is maximized, and you begin to see a pattern of overcrowding that only cable could begin to ease.

Consider Saturday afternoon football. Every other week, by and large, my home team is away. And if my home team is at home, the chances are that the neighbouring team will be away. That is how they try to work it between Chelsea and Fulham, between Liverpool and Everton, between Manchester United and Manchester City. Suppose, then, that West London cable, or Merseyside cable, or Manchester cable undertook to bring you, week by week, *Away Game*, screened as near to 'live' as made sense to the local subscribers. Here, surely, is a proper role for cable. The same principle applies to rugby, League or Union, to cricket, county or limited-over, and so on and so on. The key question, from the point of view of the non-cable-viewer, is whether such special and especially paid-for provision would rule out all or part of the coverage that he now gets for 'free'. There is an easy assumption that it would, but need it? Are there arguments that point the other way?

Televised sport is popular because network television has televised it. The corollary is that televised sport might well become less popular should network television cease to televise it. I have in mind here not simply snooker, although it is plainly true that snooker is now a lucrative and nationwide activity as a direct consequence of massive network television coverage. But in other sports steady network television exposure could build up a following that would easily outstrip the numbers of initial addicts. Motor-racing and skiing are now some way along that road. Undoubtedly, too, the presence of television cameras when Botham and Gower first took to the national cricket stage helped to revive interest in that sport. A contrary example serves to reinforce the point. Some years ago the pattern of network television football coverage was disturbed in the wake of a tussle for contracts between BBC and ITV. Television's football audiences have not fully recovered even to this day.

Today's armchair enthusiast for network sport is tomorrow's potential cable subscriber for extended service. But take away the network provision and you risk taking away the cable potential also. Remember, too, that cable provision, on any scale, is likely to be a rough and ready business. Cable coverage of a score or more away matches every footballing Saturday will not be at the same level of thoroughness as is *Match of the Day* or *The Big Match*. The Everton or Liverpool supporter will probably wear that, but for his son or his son's son the tone and style, and with them the expectation of what football on television can be like, will be set nationally by a Motson or a Moore, as it always has been. Similarly, it is no great surprise that imported televised sport always falls well behind British coverage in audience reach lacking that confirming touch of a Longhurst, a Maskell or an Arlott.

So, serious conflict between the claims of local cable and the claims of the general viewer can probably be avoided even in sport. There remains, however, one possible development that could prove seriously disruptive, and this takes us out of the world of local cable and back both to the world of network, by satellite or by satellite and cable combined and to the notion of an all-sports network. It is this prospect that gives the existing duopoly recurrent nightmares. Their networks are not as dependent on sport as critics allege, but sport is the scheduler's best friend in time of need, and a schedule that contained no sport might seem a dour and bleak affair. There follows, too, the fear that a successful raid on one key element of the service, such as sport, could lead to raids on other entertainment items, further diminishing the attraction of networks to viewers. This, it is said, would inexorably lead to a crippling loss of advertising revenue in ITV and to the loss of will to sustain the licence fee that supports the BBC.

The BBC and ITV are too easily given to pessimism. Both have demonstrated, time and again, that they are capable of fighting their way out of a tight corner, and both have been known to yield the occasional day the better to pop up elsewhere on the morrow. Our proper anxiety should always be directed not towards existing institutions, no matter how admirable they may be, but to the underpinning interests of the general viewer. The new services of satellite and cable carry both the promise of enrichment and the threat of deprivation. Accommodations there will undoubtedly have to be between the giants of broadcasting's second age and the entrepreneurs of the third, but until such time as we can see that new opportunities and services can be available to all, we must work against the grain, work to check deepening divisions between those who have access to the new and those who do not. Constant vigilance will be required, for the greatest danger is that of gradual disenfranchisement by stealth. And in basic economic terms, we are already too close for comfort to being two nations to risk heaping an avoidable broadcast apartheid on top.

2. Open Space for Arts

MELVYN BRAGG

There is a sense in which television and the arts could be regarded as antipathetic. How can the silent, private imagination of the poet and novelist, the armada of sounds from a symphony orchestra, the still settlement of a painting or the spatial exercises of ballet be crunched down to the size of a television screen and re-delivered, with any approximation to fine distinctions, on the randomly gobbling scanner? To display the subtlety and variety of forms developed in the arts, television has one instrument: a blunt box that literally diminishes the human being.

It is an argument that can be furnished with examples from every area. Painting, for instance, would seem an obvious contender, as the least difficult of the arts to transfer. Yet only rarely is any painting shot in a way that truly satisfies the artist. The inflexible proportions of the screen dictates that every shot be a rectangle. Very few paintings obey this inexorable geometry in the exact measurements demanded. Therefore the basic image on television is, more often than not, different from the artist's intention. As the size of a painting is one of the most important factors in its structure, television, from the very first shot, falls behind.

In attempts to catch up, directors use close-ups, zooms, pans and cuts—not always insensitively. The fact remains, however, that the painter's work is designed to be seen as a whole. It does not want the directorial-optical traffic control of the movies. However carefully done, this chopping up of the painting, while it might be helpful to some—and of particular use in making an academic point—is anathema to the basic intention of the work. And how long do you hold it on the screen? Some people can happily spend half an hour looking at a Rembrandt *Self-Portrait*: others might want to glance at it for a few minutes and return later for another short viewing. Once

28

again, the director has no choice but to take the decision into his own hands and determine the amount of time you will spend in front of the painting. It is he, then, who decides both what you will see and how long you will be given to see it. Too frequently he will also decide how you ought to react by plastering music all over it or manufacturing a clever juxtaposition with other images. The original contract between the painting and the viewer can easily become debased. And there are further questions, ranging from the technical difficulties of reproducing certain colour tones to the historical and intellectual minefields of the context in which the work ought to be presented.

An example that appears to have a good track record is the novel. By now, thousands of novels, good, bad and indifferent, have been adapted for television, often by extremely skilful writers, often played by actors of quality and produced by leading directors, cameramen and technicians. Dickens, Dostoevsky and Tolstoy— there have been notable adaptations from 250 years of fiction. They give great pleasure, promote the sale of the original book, often strive with painstaking ingenuity to re-invent the original for the screen, allow ample air time for the project—and yet almost always founder on what may seem to be the essence of the original: its style and 'voice'.

A set of problems arises that is different from that facing the attempt to squeeze paintings on to the screen—related, though, in the fundamental intransigence of that single screen which has to serve such a variety of purposes. For despite the most enormous care and attention, television has so far failed to deliver the novel fully. However conscientious the screenplays and adept the casting and pacing, the central characteristics that give the novel its force have slithered out of the final grasp of the programme makers. In crude instances teleplays have stripped the novel down to dialogue and action—an understandable first move—and junked the 'descriptive bits', the reflections, the authorial summaries, the important qualifications of adverb and adjective. Even when that has been avoided, however, and a more concentrated attempt made to draw on as much of the author's fiction as possible, what you are still left with, at best, is a gleaming imitation. Once more, the nature of the essential and original contract has to be broken; you make your omelette by breaking your eggs.

In its first form the novel was a complicated and sophisticated

29

private deal, written by one person alone for the enjoyment of another alone, presupposing a conjunction of pacing, the space and silence to engage and prod a private imagination and, almost above all, the willingness on the part of the reader to discover and attend to the idiosyncratic tone of mind of the writer. All this goes out of the television screenplay: even the very best work—such as John Mortimer's loving adaptation of Evelyn Waugh's *Brideshead Revisited*—failed to reconstruct that particular quality of mind that finds itself in Waugh's style and stance. It's hardly surprising. A loose and baggy monster it may be, but the novel has, from early days, been both the refuge and delight of writers fully aware of the multiplicity of responses and rewards that can be harvested from the form, a form that still yields to most of E. M. Forster's formula but also exists in a state of private play between two individuals dependent on the common recognitions of that tone of mind: style.

In other areas the antipathy between television and the arts can appear more like outright hostility. It would seem offensive and absurd to take the vast mobiles of ballet and opera and sweat them on to the small screen, mini ballerinas, midget sopranos, matchstick men all—like putting a double-decker bus through a car-crushing plant and ending up with a chunk of metal the size of a cocoa tin. A similar sweeping scorn could be directed against the transmission of orchestral music—all the resonance of ninety-six brilliant instrumentalists trickles through a sound box better suited to relaying police messages. Once again, a cluster of other disadvantages sprout up like dragons' teeth to bite the system that feeds off them: to whom, and when, and why do you cut during a performance? How do you relate the parts to the whole, the whole to the screen, the screen to the original idea?

Examples and inadequacies could be multiplied. There are those active in one or other of the arts who find this comforting. The *arriviste* stands baffled outside the gates of the old culture, and its lack of success reassures the established forms. A strong and persistent snobbery and elitism—undeniable and surely tedious to instance— reinforces these with a sense of complacency: it is right and proper, so it goes, that the vulgar mob rule of television should be repulsed. The arts are a special preserve and best kept that way.

Those of us who practise the arts and also work in television find the impenetrability of the arts, their reluctance to join in the teleflow, both impressive and daunting: that smug, ungenerous and fundamentally insensitive elitism is simply depressing and is one of the spurs that encourage us to try to make arts programmes.

There are those, though, who would side-step the entire argument by asserting that television itself, the whole ceaseless eye-bash, is, in a rumbustious, vigorous and healthily vulgar way, an 'art'. Like comics, like circuses, like the old variety music hall—but like a gigantic version of these precursors of popular art—television is the true chronicle and art-like simulacrum of our times.

Our times are times of increasing demands for mass participation: television, so far, has trained its battery on the mass. Our times are times of vivid technological advances; television flicks you across the globe by satellite, splits your screen, slows down your football, distorts your images, plays tricks with the ghosts in the machine and celebrates the gadgetry of modern inventions. Our times are times of a flood of information so great that all of us need an Ark. Television is that Ark, and it drops all the animals aboard in our sitting-rooms—news, sport, songs, battles, jokes, plays, science, ancient civilizations, gossip, lectures, comedy, agony, therapy. The whole of television could be regarded as a monstrous fiction, bringing us stories of war and society, politics and pleasure, proceeding by the laying on of strands, a seamless endless pot-pourri of electronic nights.

It is before television that almost the whole of society sits down to appreciate the skills and heroics that have always been a binding and heightening factor in any culture: world champions slug it out for us or finesse their craft with a perfection that appeases and reinforces our sense of its worth. The house is the ideal casting for a television set: it rests there, safe, snug, at your command, able to take you anywhere in the world, a magic carpet that wonderfully complements the bounded, static, mortgaged fact of bricks and mortar. The family is ideal casting for television: a related group of people constrained to live with one another, able to comment and share equally in the fantasy of a common global experience. The drive of Western society, with its constant implicit and explicit promises of more and more, is well serviced by the gobble-box that ravenously harvests both rarities and commodities. In so far as we have a common culture, that culture is transmitted through television and, to some extent, created by it. Great contests in battle and sport—not a small part of any culture's bedrock understanding of the heroics or anti-heroics that characterize its nature—are either arranged with television firmly in mind or find themselves becoming part of television willy-nilly.

In a more modest sense, television is the gossip of the day. People's references to the great event or the latest local incident are very often based on the view given them by television. There are those who would contend that such gossip is the binding culture of the time, the apparently inchoate but somehow cohesive raw matter out of which artists select and create, but always at a loss, Shakespeare being only the foremost to declare art's inferiority to nature. In appearing to take on the whole of human life and nature, and in an undisguisedly vulgar way, television—so this argument would run—is down there in the swampy, heaving mess of 'real life'. To take this a stage further, there are those who contend that there is more to be gained from watching a week's television, in terms of some of the satisfactions traditionally associated with the arts—insight into society, appreciation of the variety and individuality of humankind— than in any single contemporary artwork. Now that we have the means to meet the full spread of life (so those rejoicers in the power of the box would proclaim), the older art forms will increasingly become and look marginal. No matter that they will have presence and power for many years to come: history is stiff with corpses that many dullards thought full of life centuries after their deaths. Television is the snout of our times, they would argue, and its respiration could be seen as the way to discover the pulse of the age, a pulse most usually registered in the traditional arts; more than that, it will appear as both the inhalation and the exhalation of the day, a true artefact to our late twentieth-century times, a mirror and a window pane.

By this argument even the 'rubbish' is valuable. Indeed, some of the brightest and younger television critics find the rubbish more valuable than anything else, not only because of its crypto-Dickensian energy—although that is important, and, like many arts in their infancy, television reaches out for energy and finds it on that common ground long abandoned by many of the long-established forms—but also because it shows television at its best as a medium. There is often something identifiably better produced about a mass-viewed, slap-happy game show than there is about a 'serious' television magazine programme. The game-show producers both delight in the medium and take it for granted: they are in command of its resources and confident of the demands of pace, 'real-time' and precise delivery of an intention. Similarly, some of the soap operas are produced with an easy flair that gives them more authority on television—and certainly more proven popularity and viewability— than any number of adaptations that are forced to drag along the heaving length of other forces, other days. It is hardly surprising, perhaps, that if television is to be regarded as a popular art, then it is best suited to deal with the most popular forces. But, as we know, popular forces—like an apparently simple song lyric or a brief melody—can encapsulate a meaning of substantial resonance.

While much rubbish remains rubbish and ought to be labelled as such, the fact is not only that much in the established fields of the arts is also rubbish, but also that television, still in its early adolescence, could be said to be clearing its ground with the easier subjects, preparing itself for a more unself-conscious leap towards those difficulties that have always also been part of any work of art, clearing away the restraints of an over-respectful regard for the past. What those critics see in the zappy popular game shows and the sleek serials is television at peace with itself: in that state, undeniable pleasures and even insights are produced.

Moreover—again following this contention that all of television is one vast, populistic art—it is noticeable that some of the finest visual work has been done as 'pure' television. There are television commercials and television videos that brilliantly use the idea of image-making and projecting. Unlike photography, unlike cinema, unlike painting, unlike any of the television representations of paintings, those videos and commercials simply use television techniques to create pictures for television that will have the instant impact of a stained-glass window in a medieval church. Whether they will have as lasting a life is, of course, highly debatable but not entirely dismissible as a possibility.

Not, that is, by those who would propose the television-as-art thesis. For them, the less it feeds off the past the better: television is the ultimate discovery of the instant art of the present. Its very looseness, defects, earthiness, banality, boredom, over-indulgence and sloppiness can all be excused on two grounds: one, that this is a 'true' representation of life out there as it is; two, that it stands in a fundamentally different relationship to its material than did previous arts. It is an art that presents rather than represents. You, the viewer, are no longer in the role of passive recipient; you are now the collaborator, the selector, the cutter and shaper of your own

33

swathes of understanding through this endless acreage of matter.

It is, in several ways, a point of view.

The traditional and contemporary arts have not occupied much of television's space. In America this profile is about as high as the Utah flats. In Europe their presence is higher, but there is the generally inescapable feeling that these are cultural lumps plopped in the television soup to do you good. In Britain there have been attempts on various fronts to integrate the arts into the general system. Most of television's mass audience has remained indifferent. Cable and video may break the mass grip.

Television in this country has approached the arts in three ways: it has simply relayed them, chiefly in performances from opera houses, theatres, concert halls or studios; it has aspired to match them, most notably in the television play; and it has reported on them.

The transmission of the arts can be criticized on many grounds, all of them adding up to the overall view that television necessarily diminishes the experience—that can scarcely be argued against. Two factors militate against the glum consequence implied by that conclusion. The first is social. There are few opera houses, few ballet companies, few large orchestras: many people are not well placed to get to venues, or able to afford the expense of paying to see performances, or, equally important, able to undertake what for them would be unfamiliar and unnerving cultural pilgrimages. Television brings opera, ballet, music into the house, cheaply, and enables them to be viewed without that alteration of lifestyle that people understandably find difficult. Perhaps partly for these reasons, the minority (by British television standards, a 'minority' audience can be thought of as an audience of less than 3 million) who do watch those relays and transmissions are highly appreciative. Television's research into audience reaction (as distinct from size) always discovers a great, even fervent, sense of gratitude for the transmitted arts, despite all the limitations.

The second observation I would make has to do with the sophisticated way in which people watch television. There are many levels of watching, from the barely attentive to the totally concentrated, and games are played between the viewers and the screen, games with unwritten but discernible rules. In the case of the transmission of performances, the viewers discount the disadvantages, I think; they wipe out the expectation of their being 'like it really is', and they set up a parallel but different system of responses based on an understanding of what they are getting. In short, they look at them using their experience of looking at television as much as their experience of looking at opera or ballet. This is not to say that they expect a lesser or thinner experience: indeed, like those who prefer their football from the sofa rather than from the terraces, they may find that this television 'boxing' gives them more. They may even discover that the director's visual reading of the piece accords with their own interpretation, in which case every cut will enhance their pleasure. Whether it is out of gratitude, or that understanding of television, or a combination of both, the fact is that the relayed arts give more than a little delight to an enormous number of people (a single transmission reaches far more people than visit Covent Garden in a whole year).

(A note in parenthesis. Many of the large companies are subsidised out of taxpayers' money. The general public pays a further fee for its television. There is clearly some demand for the work of those companies to be available to a wide public. The obvious solution is to put them on tape for the television screen via the networks or video. Educationalists and enthusiasts guarantee audiences large enough to give a sense of fair return for those initial subsidies and licences. Yet the expense of taking a production from any of the subsidised companies is quite extraordinarily high—even by television's own costly standards—and is becoming prohibitive. Surely a combination of pressure from the Arts Council and the broadcasting institutions could persuade the companies and their unions to lower the demanded fees, accept a proportion in deferred royalties and at least permit the productions to be recorded and made available. I have suggested that this be discussed and moved forward on several occasions and have been met with goodwill and inertia. It is, though, a disgrace that the very high fees being demanded by companies whose money comes from the taxpayer should prevent recordings being made that would, at the very least, let the taxpayer see where his money was going.)

One area of transmitted television that can have few detractors is that of monumental and museum culture. To be able to see the great Hindu temples of India, the city of Kiyoto, the pyramids of Mexico and treasures from palaces in Arabia and Europe—the mere sight of them, however reduced they are—is thrilling. Once again, it is not too difficult to make an adjustment similar to the one we make when

35

we buy postcard-size reproductions of favourite paintings: they are not the real thing, but they are unarguably much better than nothing and by no means negligible in their own right. In that sense, by simply recording the records of the past, television performs a thoroughly defensible and often enjoyable service.

Television has aspired to become a peer in the house of arts most successfully and consistently through the original television play. Certain films about artists could claim to be 'art', a cross between the art movie and the literary biography; certain documentaries, especially from the natural history producers, give off reverberations and seem to carry that particular combination of force and grace that gives them a fair claim to being described as 'art'. But it is in the television play and the television comedy that most certainty can be placed. The play is also the only one of the three areas being discussed here—the other two being the transmitted arts and the reported arts—that enters into the mass-audience market.

Perhaps that is one of the clues. The television play was born of a determination among a number of British playwrights in the late 1950s to speak to the television audience without benefit of theatrical pre-production or previously confirmed theatrical success. They wrote for the screen, and they had to discover not only what the technical possibilities were but at what target the tube was aimed. In brief, they had to become part of the television production team—an outfit with plenty of its own faults and pot-holes of inadequacy, but nevertheless a comparatively ordered contemporary crew with engineering and mechanical skills as well as directing and writing abilities. By working properly with television they made plays for television that did not suffer from the flaws of adaptation or bear the strains of reinterpreting. Not only has British television allowed an impressive number of playwrights both to write good plays and to reach an audience whose nearest equivalent is the audience for Victorian fiction (and the interplay between television playwrights, their audience and their subject matter bears a remarkable similarity to that earlier age), but it has also encouraged those whose more natural home is the novel or the stage to come aboard, again often very successfully. David Mercer and Dennis Potter are two fine examples of original television playwrights; John Osborne, Tom Stoppard and Harold Pinter are dramatists whose work for television has had no less integrity than their work for the stage. The *Monty Python* team and the *Not the Nine O'Clock News* team have shown how brilliantly TV and comedy can combine. This could well be claimed as television's most important contribution to the contemporary arts.

The third arm of television's relationship with the arts—reporting on the arts—has been largely unsatisfactory. There has never been enough of it; it has rarely had a chance to develop a momentum; it has often been done ineptly. Compared with the vast coverage of the arts in daily and weekly newspapers and magazines, in generalized and specialist journals and on the radio, television's record is poor.

Take the case of books as one example. As I write this piece, there is not a single regular book programme on any of the three networked channels, nor have plans yet been announced for a regular book programme on Channel Four. In this country—where there are over 700 million library borrowings annually from public libraries alone, where hundreds of books are reviewed in a year's pages of quite modest journals, where a fair crop of young poets, novelists, historians and writers can still have a sporting chance of being published if not in hardback or paperback, then in one of the many metropolitan or provincial literary magazines, where some leaders of the political parties and other institutions (including broadcasting) do read books, even review books or at least like to be caught with a quote or a photograph in front of leather bindings—this consistent neglect could be thought of as both perplexing and scandalous.

Consequently, to attempt a serious discussion of television and books is to risk cross-examining an absent witness. But there have been three methods of approach. Programmes have attempted to match the review pages by bringing reviewers into the studio and simply asking them to speak what would be better written. Developments of this idea have included programmes that have used the television discussion format to pursue a reviewing purpose. The second method has been the interview with the author, the third a more considered film profile of the author.

The attempt to review books has worked well only intermittently, principally because of the shortage of space allotted to those programmes. With half an hour a week for a run of thirteen weeks, there is just not the time to proffer reviewing that in any way matches the richness of the available material. Therefore from the outset the programmes have tended to become either insufferably busy and fragmented—however enjoyable—or stonily aware that by reviewing one or two books they are only emphasizing how many they are not reviewing. And after eight or thirteen weeks the schedule axe has fallen and book programmes have been 'rested'. Book reviewing could work on television. It could even work with about forty-five minutes a week. But unless and until there is a proper commitment to such programmes, and a commitment that stretches through fifty-two weeks, they will come and go like fair-weather friends and never either settle down or yield up their possibilities.

The straight author interview has often worked quite well. The difficulties are obvious: some authors respond reluctantly to the format of the interview, and their reluctance is understandably compounded when they find themselves ambushed by a menacingly encircling television crew. A book is a book is a book. It exists between the first and the last page. Attempts at explanation may be interesting, but they are rarely more than semaphore signals from a man who never wanted to talk with flags. If the book under discussion is a current work—which means that few of the audience will be acquainted with it—then the interview has to carry the burden of displaying the plot, the themes, the characters, the book's wares, as well as engaging the writer in a conversation that has for him the flavour of chewed cud. Despite that, the interview, particularly the longer interview, appears to satisfy a large number of those who watch. The mere sight of the author himself is not to be underestimated as a force of attraction: whatever the question asked, the viewer can make up his mind about the man—as much from the silences as the responses, as much from the manner as the matter— simply by observing him in close-up for forty or fifty minutes.

The most satisfactory programme, in my opinion, is that which combines all three elements by focusing on a particular book at the publicly correct time in the author's career, thereby gaining from the audience's overall readiness (through the agency of other media) to engage with the subject; by using the interview; and by adding an essay line that reinforces the interview, centres on the new publication, includes themes and variations from other works and puts all these together in the best television film/documentary tradition.

An example would be a film made with and about William Golding to coincide with the publication of *Rites of Passage*. It was decided to concentrate on three of Golding's novels, *Lord of the Flies*, *The Spire* and *Rites of Passage*, and to draw themes from those novels that could be illustrated by interviewing the author and reinforced by readings from his essays, apposite biographical material and appropriate location shooting. Thus—an obvious instance—that part of the film dealing with *The Spire* was set in the Close of Salisbury Cathedral, at the foot of the monument that had triggered and catalysed the book. When the combination of elements was properly struck, it allowed, in my opinion, a revelation of Golding and his work that was both interesting and specific to television. Near the opening of the film for example, we wanted to establish Golding's attitude to class and his approach to *Lord of the Flies*. The class theme was illustrated by a pan across the town of Marlborough (where he had been brought up), accompanied by Golding's voice dissecting the class/income structure of the town. We then had Golding talking about his politically and intellectually active parents—photographs of them were a useful confirmation of his description—and a visit to his childhood house, where, through anecdotes, he placed his own class position in the town and the time exactly, and further, again through anecdote, indicated his own sense of the weight of the forces of the past most graphically and simply. He spoke of his education at Oxford, an early volume of poetry and the unsuccessful writing based both on the socialist optimism of his parents and on his own more puzzled appreciation of life, and from there moved on to the Second World War. He described how during that war he changed his view of human nature. To see him talking about this was compelling. The idea that interviews are 'radio' is ridiculous: the sight of someone talking intently is an undeniably rich experience. Post-war, then marriage, children, the hemmed-in life of a schoolmaster, bedtime reading for the children, books, all of which at one stage seemed to be about brave British boys on islands. He described how one night he had told his wife that someone ought to write a 'real' book about boys on islands. She encouraged him. Six weeks saw the first draft done while he was still teaching and spending much time in the Cathedral with the boys rehearsing in the choir. . . . I have left out a lot of the detail, but in about ten minutes of screen time a rich mix was assembled and organized that allowed the viewers to appreciate Golding's background, the change of his views, his method of thought and work, the circumstances of his first novel and its location in his life. If it were possible to persuade the institutional powers that programmes such as this could and should be attempted at least once a week, television could begin to establish firm ground, and on its own terms, as an observer/interpreter of contemporary literature.

Everything written about the paucity of the coverage of books can be applied, *mutatis mutandis*, to the theatre, to the visual and plastic arts, to dance, music (classical, rock and jazz), design, photography and television itself. Steady, regular and attentive coverage is just not there. Such semi-regular arts programmes as there are (and not one of them runs throughout the year: the *South Bank Show*, with the longest run, is off the air for five months a year) start out with a burden of responsibilities and ambitious intentions that they know will increase as the debt of what is undone piles up. The only solution, in the circumstances, is to establish a definite limitation for the programme, work to it and work also to claim other slots. The single most constraining factor in television arts programmes is lack of space: it constantly threatens to disable the programmes so that they are prevented from reflecting in rich and various ways the abundance of activity that they are purposefully designed to embrace. Lack of space tends to inhibit the employment of a critical approach: as there are so few slots, the thinking goes, it is simply a waste not to use most of it on revelation and illumination. This gives many programmes the appearance of being monotonously celebratory. Lack of space inhibits experiment and the taking on of more obscure work, for arts programmes have almost always felt, with good cause, that as the present system is organized, they are merely tolerated and have to prove their reliability without fail. Lack of space cramps the possibility of illustration that could enrich the programme and extend both its availability and its range. Lack of space has forced those who want to report on the arts to resort to impact rather than appreciation as the most effective way to make a mark. Cable could change this.

It would be unfair to paint a picture of unqualified gloom. Millions of people have enjoyed ballets, operas, plays, concerts and whole cultures that have been brought to them through television. No essay on television and the arts should fail to mention Kenneth Clark's *Civilization*—its commendable ambition and its encouragement to the institutions to risk lengthy and overall assessments—ballet months, opera months, performances from Covent Garden and Glyndebourne, craft series, series on paintings, competitions (most notably the Young Musician of the Year). All of these have given the arts a presence on the screen that, in audience terms, could be said to outweigh their general popularity. In that sense, the institutions might claim they have done well enough by the arts.

Regular reporting on the arts has come through the more generalised current affairs programmes or through clearly labelled arts programmes. In the early 1950s it was not uncommon for BBC's *Panorama* to include items on the arts, a brief taken over by the *Tonight* programme and continued, though partially, through the 1960s and 1970s. At present *Newsnight* on BBC-2 carries a regular arts reporter. I have always thought that there was a great deal to be said for planting the arts firmly in current affairs. At the very least, it would give them a place in what television regards as the serious side of things; there is always the danger that the specialist arts programmes will carry the stigma of the conscience box. I would go further—indeed, I have tried and have so far failed—and attempt to encourage the inclusion of arts news on the news bulletins. Sport, for example, which is not as well attended as the performing arts, is part of almost every newscast of the day. It would be difficult initially, but not inconceivable, for an arts editor on a news programme to build up the public presence of his subject area as sports editors do. (It is hard to resist the reflection that in this respect the news clearly reveals the tastes and interests of the newsmen rather than those of the audience.) There is some hope that Channel Four might attempt this—but it will work only if it is persisted with. Too many promising ideas about the arts have been killed off because they were not given the time to take root inside the system and in the viewing pattern of the audience. The downside of a defensible claim by the television institutions that they have given the arts more time than their popularity merits is that they have required them to prove themselves over-quickly and have designated them, often unnecessarily, as 'treats' to be withdrawn almost at will or in times that they regard as tough.

Specialist arts programmes were set out on their course by Sir Huw Wheldon's *Monitor* on the BBC. In the late 1950s and early 1960s he virtually had the field to himself, and the celebratory tone which has characterized so many arts programmes since is understandable, indeed unavoidable, with such subjects as Robert Graves, Ben Shahn, Marcel Duchamp, Ezra Pound, Giulini and Benjamin Britten making their first appearances on television. Wheldon's skill in choosing his team resulted in memorable programmes and the early establishment of ways of making arts programmes: the illustrated interview, the process film, the 'art' film biography (most memorably on Elgar), the quirky/oblique director slot, the overall and undisguised intention to educate through television story-telling. Kenneth Tynan's *Tempo*, on ITV, attempted a more frontal attack on the contemporary arts, Tynan employing his own taste and involvement as an involved critic to direct the programme towards what he saw as the best of the time.

Since the early 1960s arts programmes have included Jonathan Miller's *Monitor*; *Omnibus*, edited successively by Stephen Hearst, Norman Swallow, Mike Wooller and Leslie Megahay; *Second House*, edited by Bill Morton; *Aquarius*, edited by Humphrey Burton; *Review*, edited by Lorna Pegram and Colin Nears; book programmes edited by Will Wyatt, Robert Robinson and myself; Gavin Millar's and Barry Norman's film programmes; *The Old Grey Whistle Test* for rock; and a fair number of regional arts programmes on both BBC and ITV. At the time of writing the BBC carries Christopher Martin's *Onibus* on BBC-1; *Arena*, edited by Alan Yentob, is on BBC-2; the *South Bank Show*, which I edit, is on ITV. None of them—as is worth repeating, I think—is transmitted for longer than six or seven months. Apart from those networked programmes, several BBC regions and ITV companies carry local arts programmes. Channel Four promises to make a substantial addition to this output.

Lumped together in a paragraph, it can seem to be reasonably impressive. Certainly, out of these series have come programmes memorable to the public and influential within the industry. The scarcity of space has often concentrated the minds of producers and forced them towards essays in style—from the exploration of leisurely pacing to concern with the power of detail—that have extended the possibilities of programme-making. Those with whom I work, for instance, are attempting to develop the idea of constructing programmes that carry a critique as well as a description and celebration of the subject. Certain areas, such as the process film, to take just one example, are constantly reworked, and some of the rewards for long and intensive attention are now evident. There is no doubt that there is a great deal of ground to cover, and there exists the will and the talent to cover it more rigorously and more entertainingly. What we need most of all, though, is more space; while Channel Four will provide that to some degree, it is the imminence of cable television that could signal the quantum leap.

Cable ought to provide two things: direct access for that minority that prefers arts programmes to other forms of programming, and the air time for such programmes to breathe properly at last. If the cable systems do spread as widely and as remorselessly as is sometimes anticipated, the effect will be not unlike that of the decentralization and deregulation of book publishing, as it passed from the monopolistic hands of the Church to the enormous variety of lay publishers. At the moment in this country two central bodies contain and control electronic publishing. What is seen is decided by them. Until the invention of the video tape, when it was seen was also in their hands. The video both releases the audience from the bondage of scheduling and gives television writers and producers that possible link with durability, respectability and posterity that they have always hankered after and felt diminished through the lack of. Cable could further release the arts audience (and, of course, other minority audiences) from the tyranny of programme placing, which often means that the programmes they want to watch are on too late and/or up against films and other programmes in which they have a competing interest. If the cable system develops as its enthusiasts predict, then, at last, television will be able to provide a multiplicity of outlets comparable with that enjoyed in print journalism and publishing. America is well under way with the first phase.

For this article I looked into the ABC Arts cable system. This has the support of the major American network channel, although so far its budget is pygmy by comparison. Nevertheless, this is part of their policy. Twenty-one hours a week are transmitted, three hours a night. The content is exclusively the visual and performing arts. Operas are transmitted from Covent Garden and Shakespeare from the Lincoln Centre; Joe Papp's New York Festival Theatre contributes a regular band of plays; jazz has a settled slot; a young generation of choreographers and photographers has been brought in; established directors, such as Robert Altman, have directed plays for the channel; link-ups have been established with museums, notably the Metropolitan Museum in New York and the Walker Art Centre in Minneapolis.

The system at present reaches 6.5 million homes. Recently, a 'call number' was introduced on to the screen, and viewers were asked for their comments. So far the calls are running at 600 per night, all but unanimously favourable and grateful for the opportunity to see the material. Critical response—in the *New York Times*, for instance, and the arts journals—has been very positive and welcoming. So far, so good.

The worry is finance. As Mary-Ann Tighe of ABC Arts explained to me, advertisers are simply not used to a specialized television audience; the agencies have never before attempted to cope with a television audience that is not promised as a fat fraction of the mass. They do not know how to redirect their campaigns; nor, I suspect, are they yet finally convinced that such redirection would be profitable. It could be a race against the economic clock. Can the cable networks survive and prove themselves for long enough and well enough to convince and re-educate the advertisers, whose support is, ultimately, vital?

It would be a disaster for minority television if advertisers were not to recognize this for the opportunity it is. A minority that is fully attentive to the screen and could, in the USA, number between 5 and 15 million, carries considerable purchasing potential. To know that you were definitely reaching a specific target group, and one as alert as those telephone calls suggest, ought to be a cause more for celebration than caution. Television advertising, though, has been so rigidly aimed at the mass market for so long that it may be suffering from the rigor mortis that afflicts many unreservedly successful enterprises.

For the future health of television arts programmes cable has to succeed. The present system—despite its outstanding successes and the regular evidence of decent effort—presses towards compromise or a selectivity so necessarily refined that it threatens to appear arbitrary and whimsical.

What I shall regret, should cable become so powerful as to strip the networks of their nerve or capacity to deliver minority programmes, is the end of the relationship with the mass audience. For although television arts programmes are watched by a minority, only a percentage of that minority comprises regular and committed viewers; the larger part of it is the usual mix—heavy viewers, irregular viewers, lazy viewers, occasional viewers, curious viewers, the mix that watches most other programmes. This generalized 'scatter' audience has been both a curse and a motivating force. The attempt to reach out to it has often provoked understandable mockery. It risks being patronizing and populist and is shallow. Yet, taken properly into account, the audience can help programmes towards the clarity and generosity of intention that has characterized many great works of the past (Shakespeare's audience, Dickens's public and Picasso's following being only three of a number of similar instances).

The knowledge that 'out there' is a public, a large proportion of which now absorbs the greater part of its information and entertainment from television, is one of the sustaining reasons for the commitment of many of those who work in television arts. It comes from a rooted satisfaction in the widespread availability of television and its freedom from association with established social, economic and educational habits and systems that have so often cut off whole classes and regions from any wide-ranging contact with the arts.

There are two stages in trying to reach this general audience. One is to provide information at the top of the programme that, as it were, brings them up to the scratch line. The obvious has to be grasped. This introduction can usefully be continued into the first few minutes of the film. From then on the integrity of the subject and the producer's intentions must group around a narrative clarity that has to find ways of continuing to spin out that initial thread of connection. In many ways this can be an extremely useful discipline, not entirely unlike the use of plot in literary story-telling. The best arts programmes I have seen have always succeeded in that difficult simplicity of line. Even such an unlikely contender as a long interview can be kept within these bounds—by the inclusion of information within questions, by discreet interpolative explanation—and the bounds in most cases prove a fertile set of constraints.

It would be a pity if we were to let slip that part of the programme's thinking that addresses itself to people who are interested, even enthusiastic, but not well informed. Although it might seem a release, it could also prove the trigger for a disastrous slither into self-indulgence or, more likely, a preparedness to be satisfied solely with esoteric attention. That the diversification to be brought about by cable might enable a great deal of specialization and more in-depth examination is to be anticipated with pleasure: if it knocks out entirely a concern for the general audience, it could well lose one of its richest seams.

The outlook for television and the arts looks optimistic. There are those who see this time as providing the opportunity for European treasures, and principally British expertise, to launch a massive assault on the world market. We have a comparatively large number

45

of people experienced in the complex and often Byzantine business of arts programme-making, which includes everything from dealing with international superstars as celebrated for their temperaments and fees as for their talent, to squaring opera houses, unions and international agreements—besides all of which the construction and execution of a programme often seems a tranquil sport. The markets are opening up not only in cable but also in video disc, cassette and satellite. It is not inconceivable that the next decade could see arts productions increase between two- and ten-fold.

As arts programmes move towards areas in which they can reach target audiences, not only will they be required in greater quantities but they will also probably call into play a secondary set of characteristics, until now largely ignored or disdained by British programme-makers: those of the selling operation. If arts programmes make enough of an impact to create a true sense of a connected community attuned to television presentation, then more sophisticated productions will also breed richer representations: the messages 'Go and enjoy', 'Go and see', 'Go and do' will be hammered home across the hoardings on the television screen. At present the restricted operating area of the arts rightly spurns that sort of hard-selling; a bigger and more open system would be able to carry it, and, in its wider context, that need be no bad thing.

One final area—provenly successful but up until now explored only sparingly—that could benefit enormously from these changes is that of participation. When we ran a poetry competition, a couple of years ago, for example, more than 35,000 poems arrived in our office; out of those came winners and an impressive anthology. Whenever competitions have been properly launched, the response has been substantial, often overwhelming. A great number of people are interested enough in the arts to want to join in. Many of them find the only way is through a large public competition. This involvement would immeasurably enrich the programme–audience relationship so often inaccurately described as 'passive'. In this instance 'more widely available' could mean 'richer'. A popular art form could make an important contact with its popular audience and recycle what it has teased out.

I started by arguing the case for the gap between television and the traditional arts. It is a case that I am always aware of but have spent my professional life in television attempting to undermine. A fair number of the most resourceful and organized talents in British television have devoted themselves to this attempt, sometimes quixotically, sometimes ineptly, but successfully on enough occasions to provide precedents for continuing action. Whatever successes there have been owe a lot to the existing structures of British television, both BBC and ITV. Plant, funds, expertise, air time, the right to fail—these have been made available, if not often enough, at least in sufficient quantity for a start and a mark to be made. The context of British television, with its huge production houses and internal cross-benefits, has helped, at its best, to lash the arts to the taxing demands of a medium so often ill-understood and lightly dismissed by those whose skills and visions have led them into the more acceptable and established forms. The chance, in this time of transition, is that greater opportunities for the making of programmes will educate more artists into television, will build on the best of what has been done here and will encourage the expansion and export of programmes that in themselves sit increasingly comfortably alongside the work they portray. More space and more markets could, with luck, close the gap.

3. News Overkill

PETER IBBOTSON

The video revolution is about entertainment. That is the message of the new video shops and the nightmare of the network controllers. It is also the verdict of the Government's Information Technology Advisory Panel, which has recommended the development of thirty cable channels, of which twenty would be devoted to entertainment. Cassette, satellite broadcasting and the wiring of our cities are sure to bring about rapid changes in what we see and where we see it. Sport, feature films and perhaps much light entertainment may be bought by the highest bidder and may disappear from the traditional channels to reappear on cassette or, by special and expensive subscription, via cable or satellite. This is overwhelmingly the chief area of concern, debate and commercial opportunity: programmes of entertainment and diversion are the cutting edge of the coming upheaval of television as we have known it.

But what about the rest? What about the acres of news and current affairs that at present make up about 12 per cent of the programmes on offer from the BBC and the ITV companies? Will they go on much as before, as a form of increasingly expensive public service? Or would an explosion of new channels sound the death-knell of their monopoly of television journalism? Will there, in the end, be any profit in these areas? And will the very multiplicity of channels offer a real widening of the freedom of expression? Whether or not the Cup Final is on BBC or cable will be an early and noisy battle of the video revolution. How news and comment survive or develop will be a later, quieter, but perhaps more fundamental concern.

I suppose a man from Mars would find the way in which we presently run our television, and particularly our factual television, rather odd. He might note that we seem to take a fairly relaxed attitude as far as the printed word is concerned. We permit the

48

publication and distribution of newspapers, books and magazines that represent a fairly wide range of opinion and, indeed, truthfulness. There is, it is true, no prescriptive right to the freedom to publish—we have no First Amendment. There are D-notices, laws about libel, contempt and blasphemy. And the economics of publishing might be held to create a bias in the printed word in favour of the possessors of wealth. But print does cover the waterfront of opinion; it is as free as may be of authoritarian interference and, in a free market, readily adapts and changes as public demand dictates. It also comes in a range of shapes and sizes, from the *Encyclopaedia Britannica* to handbills advertising political meetings. We are so used to the variety and sheer volume of print, its freedom from the censoring hand of authority, that we take it almost completely for granted.

Our Martian observer might approve of this valuable state of affairs, but, turning to broadcasting, he would be faced by an immediate and bewildering paradox. Why, if we all have, in principle, freedom to write and publish what we will, is broadcasting rationed, hedged around with rules and restrictions and effectively operated by a very small number of professional practitioners? Why are only two institutions, the BBC and the IBA, licensed to broadcast? And why will they be providing, at the end of 1982, only four television channels? There are three reasons, two openly stated, the third hidden.

First, rationing results from the scarcity of airwaves. Whereas an infinite number of printing presses could produce an infinite number of books and newspapers at the same time, broadcasting (so far) is restricted by the limited number of frequencies that do not interfere with each other. What better reason for a state-controlled licence to broadcast? Second, there is rationing by cost: television is extravagant with time, talent and the elaborate array of technical equipment needed to produce it. Is it not better, therefore, to protect centres of excellence and not spread the jam too thin? Thirdly, and more secretly, is the preference of authority for a system that is regulated and ultimately subject to political controls. However strong its impartiality and self-esteem, British broadcasting is in its origins a political creation: it is widely felt to be the most potent form of communication in the land, and it would be surprising if those in authority viewed with total equanimity the dismantling of the system of licences, controls and reference that has been developed over the past few decades.

But now, in the 1980s, the era of rationed broadcasting faces its end. The 'scarcity of airwaves' defence crumbles in the face of the new technology. If it is possible to provide, by cable and satellite, forty channels, why should Government feel it necessary to license broadcasting authorities as a guarantee of impartiality and fairness? Could any governmental authority even begin to monitor the programmes that appeared on so many different outlets? And while there might be no certainty that the factual programmes produced by so many channels would necessarily cover all points of view, wouldn't there be a greater chance of more views being heard? Wouldn't politicians, in fact, become a little more relaxed about television journalism if there were more of it, and from many more sources? It may be that, viewed in the year 2000, the licensed duopoly of broadcasting that we take to be the natural order of things will seem as quaint and curious as the salt monopoly of James I, and just as indefensible.

The argument of cost is much more persuasive. Television is expensive. News and current affairs, particularly at the international level, are very costly. Might it not be, therefore, that the sport and entertainment and feature films that look like being the vanguard of the new channels will remain their staple fare? Might we inherit a future in which we tune to the BBC or the ITV franchise holders for our traditional news and factual programmes but switch to cable, cassette or whatever for our entertainment? Free from institutional habit and duty or legal requirement, why should any commercial broadcaster bother with anything but the most immediately attractive and profitable programming he can produce?

America is already well into the cable revolution, and its effect on news programming has been a considerable surprise to the broadcasters. The only examples so far of news production outside the existing systems are Ted Turner's two cable News Network channels based in Atlanta, Georgia, available to cable subscribers throughout the United States. Ted Turner—the so-called 'Mouth of the South'—already had a highly profitable television station, WTBS, which makes upwards of $5 million yearly. In 1980 he launched an entirely new concept, an exclusively news and factual feature channel for use by the rapidly expanding legion of cable operators, bypassing and competing with the traditional fare of CBS, NBC and ABC. The outlay on new studios, equipment, staffing and so on was enormous, totalling about $20 million, plus an annual estimated running budget of perhaps $25–$30 million. This was Cable News Network (CNN). In its first year the losses were high, and the established networks relaxed. But, by the standards of the competition, the programmes were good, and CNN managed a succession of scoops and controversial reports that made its name. By the beginning of 1982 CNN had met its break-even target: it had reached over 10 million American homes and was starting to make the profits that Ted Turner had forecast. Never one to stand still, Turner then launched his second channel, CNN-2.

The popularity of news has been a shock. Although Turner's channel is not exclusively all-news in the sense that it might be defined in Britain—there is a good deal of sport, news analysis, business features and so on—its output is nonetheless far removed from the preponderantly entertaining programmes that the three main American networks have usually offered. It is, in Ted Turner's words 'counter-programming'. But why should such a strong public appetite have been concealed for so long in a society devoted to the commercial pursuit and satisfaction of popular tastes? And why did it come right for Ted Turner? The reasons are obviously complex, but CNN seems to have benefited from three factors.

First, there is the development of new production technologies that have made news coverage both easier and more exciting. Backpack cameras, quick videotape in place of slow film, faster communications and satellite links have made a lot of news more immediate and interesting; far more is now transmitted live. Ted Turner leads the field in giving open-ended coverage of important events, while the networks are locked into their restrictive schedules. Second, the long anxiety of the Iranian hostage crisis in 1979–81 is held to have stimulated the public demand for news just as these novelties were becoming available. (We should remember that large areas of the USA have no quality daily newspaper.) And, third, Ted Turner was able to offer a good deal to cable operators hungry for material: he charged them 15 to 20 cents monthly per subscriber for the service, for which they expected audiences and hence advertising revenue. And as a bonus they satisfied the requirement to provide programmes 'in the public interest'.

The established networks, CBS, NBC and ABC, are now taking notice. They are planning to extend their news output with new factual programmes in the unused hours between midnight and

5 a.m. (with the astonishing expectation of an audience of up to 20 per cent of the population) and are leaning heavily on the all-powerful affiliate stations throughout the country to take more news and comment. On the cable front, ABC and Westinghouse have started two all-news channels, which will be offered free to cable operators. The first of these satellite news channels runs news headlines, sport, weather and features on a revolving thirty-minute repeat basis: 'Give us 18 minutes,' they boast, 'and we'll give you the world.' The second channel offers more in-depth coverage, longer items, more analysis. The start-up costs for the two channels have been put at around $40 million, and the moves of CBS and NBC are now being watched with considerable interest.

But is the discovery of an unsuspected American pool of news addicts relevant to what will happen here? Perhaps it is a passing American fad; perhaps the market will suffer overkill once all three networks start competing with CNN for the cable audience. While it is too early to make predictions about these volatile matters, we might more soberly reflect on the economic differences of news-funding in Britain and the United States.

Each of the three American networks is reckoned to spend about $150 million a year on its news operations: they can clearly afford to experiment in cable and to take the calculated risk that Ted Turner's operation is repeatable at a profit. In Britain our two existing television news organizations, BBC TV News and ITN, work with much fewer resources: a proportion of material regularly comes via the American networks, and protracted foreign stories like the Falklands crisis can put an enormous strain on budgets. They may well, though, be able to duplicate part of their output in a form better suited to cable programming. Indeed, so fervent seems the desire of the politicians that British cable should not become a total free-for-all that a basic operating requirement might be the commitment to take a recognized news service. How BBC TV News or ITN would organize the conflict of interests between their broadcast and cable customers would be an interesting institutional question.

But it is clear that Britain offers rather less attractive inducements to would-be Ted Turners. The market is smaller; the cabling will be slower; and hence the making of profits sufficient to sustain an expensive new news-gathering and processing service much less certain. That may be an unduly pessimistic outlook, but it will be a brave entrepreneur who takes that major gamble. What may happen instead is the provision of a much simpler all-day news service on cable television. As the old adage goes, news is dear, comment cheap. Such a service would offer the simplest of news headlines, bought in from the international news agencies and simply read (or even displayed) in a studio, and would be supplemented perhaps with interviews, comment and discussion. Already a number of cable channels in Amsterdam take the basic UPI/Reuter wire service as a simple visual display. Such an operation would cost a basic minimum of the subscription to the agency, plus simple television facilities, or an increase in price through a whole array of extra features, while remaining far cheaper than the full-blown news operation as we now see it on our screens.

I think that even this simple departure from our traditional view of news would prove popular. News on our present networks gets consistently high audiences (though current affairs does not). It is thought that most of us use news programmes as a sort of check-up to find out once or more each day what has happened in the world at home or abroad that might affect us. I suspect that the hard bulletins, the top-of-the-programme headlines, are what most people tune in for at nine or ten o'clock each evening: these are what satisfies our need to know. It seems curious, though, that this ritual has developed into a sort of national family prayers at fixed prime times in the early and middle part of the viewing evening. It is even more curious that news bulletins have turned into magazine programmes, with their own created celebrities, the newsreaders. This is surely a function of limited air time, for there is no overwhelming reason why news should be prepared and offered only at particular times if more hours of broadcasting were available. Perhaps we have developed a totally artificial form of news broadcasting as a result of these limitations, one that might disappear when its hard core and staple—what has actually happened—is more freely available at the touch of a button. There is no iron law that limits news on television to its three or so outings each day. The need to cram everything into the presently available formats, the need to present news as half-hour television programmes, the problems of editing and condensation, all these may disappear in a more diverse and pluralist broadcasting environment. However slow the public may be to relinquish its present loyalty to current news fare, cable news will come and will have an effect. Controllers of network television might well ponder the implications for their evening schedules.

The other forms of factual programming that we've grown used to on British television over the past thirty years or so will also come under pressure from the multiplication of channels, although in rather different ways. We have a curious form of television called 'current affairs'. America has 'public affairs' programmes, most notably the weekend press conference style of interviewing, but all daily output of comment and analysis tends to share the label 'news'. It may be that the news explosion on television across the Atlantic also caters to an increasing appetite for what we call 'current affairs', but I'm not sure that this is really the case or, if it is, that the phenomenon is waiting to be discovered here. Documentaries, it is true, are and always have been popular. *Horizon, 40 Minutes* and others are in a tradition of British television that has always attracted sizeable and appreciative audiences. Their content lasts longer than that of current affairs programmes; they can be viewed with profit and pleasure for some time after their original production; and they seem guaranteed a long life on television, whether on cassette, cable or network. But current affairs proper is usually perishable: it feeds off current events, has only brief relevance and lacks the immediate pull of news itself. Since we have created a special category for this form of broadcasting, we can only blame ourselves for the public's reaction to it, which is not over-enthusiastic. Audience research has consistently testified to much smaller audiences for current affairs programmes like *Panorama* or *TV Eye* than for straight news programmes. The ones that do best in terms of audience size, like *Nationwide*, are often those that have adopted a news-style format. Without their sympathetic placing in the schedules, many current affairs programmes would undoubtedly have far fewer viewers. More ominously, research from Sweden and Belgium has shown that as the number of channels increases, so the audience for current affairs rapidly declines as the public learns how to weave in and out of a number of schedules to find other programmes that it prefers. Serious current affairs is likely to be a loser, and those of us who have produced it may have to face up to the real level of audience appetite for it in a free market. Additionally, the traditional forms of extended foreign film reportage are again too expensive to be attractive to commercial operators taking a risk with a new cable channel. Why should they invest money in producing a half-hour film on the Common Agricultural Policy when they could more cheaply buy a bigger audience with programmes on cookery or gardening? In short, it's a question of double jeopardy: the more channels there are available, the smaller the audience that may want to watch the more demanding factual programmes and the fewer the number of controllers who will want to commission such programmes.

That, of course, is to look at the worst case. However many cable channels feed into the wired cities of the future, the existing broadcasters will be around for some time. It may well be that if the BBC loses serious parts of, say, its traditional sports coverage either to cable or to satellite, then it will have more time for documentary and current affairs programmes. Factual programming of an unashamedly public-service nature could become its singular contribution in a sea of cabled entertainment. Also, one must recognize that commercial gain may be the overriding but not necessarily exclusive motive for programme-making. Clearly, many cable operators of the future will be in business simply to provide the cheapest product for the greatest number of subscribers: as with a good deal of American television, the product is a captive part of a commercial equation. But there are also certain to be other potential producers whose desire to make and transmit television programmes stems from other motives.

For years British television has enjoyed and endured a variety of criticisms. In the area of news and current affairs in particular it has been felt to be simultaneously too radical, too Establishment, pro-Arab, pro-Israeli and so on. In other words, it has suffered from the privilege of monopoly: too many people have felt excluded from it; too many people have felt their views to be unrepresented or distorted. Unlike the press, British television has sought constantly to balance opinion, to umpire argument. Some critics, notably the Glasgow Media Group, have endeavoured to prove that this attempt at impartiality has been little more than a conspiracy against the working class and the trade unions; that the broadcasting duopoly has excluded entire rafts of opinion and information from proper public attention or, at the very least, has dealt with them only through distortion. Whether one agrees with this analysis in whole or in part, or indeed rejects it entirely, there is a strong case to be made that those who subscribe to it should have access to broadcasting. The new technology, and the dilution of the two great licensed monopolies, should provide the proper opportunity for this. If we believe in freedom of speech, expression and communication, why should we not be able to make television programmes reflecting our particular views of society and politics, just as we might write books or articles? If our carefully monitored three (and soon four) channels are multiplied tenfold and more, why shouldn't that development be accompanied by an immediate and stimulating widening of access to the medium? Politics apart, the old hierarchies and career structures of television would surely benefit from a massive infusion of new skills, new enthusiasm and new energy.

In his McTaggart Lecture at the Edinburgh Television Festival in 1981, Peter Jay took a look into the far future of cable possibilities and sketched out a science fiction scenario for electronic publishing. Every home wired for cable would be able to summon an immense variety of programmes: information, entertainment, news, sport or whatever. These would be produced on a speculative basis by whoever wished to make them and could afford the initial costs of production. The Militant Tendency might produce its own programme, as might the National Front or the Mother's Union. A meter on the set would faithfully record which programmes had been watched each week or month. The cable company—that is, the owner of the wires—would then bill each customer on a programme-by-programme basis, rather like submitting a very detailed telephone bill, and would pass on to producers (after deduction of profits and expenses) the money that their programmes had generated. This, it is argued, would be as close an equivalent to free publishing as television could achieve: freedom of access limited only by the normal laws hedging the published word, commercial success dependent on the willingness of the public to buy. And marketing by cable would surely be easier than the distribution of print.

But is the Jay prospect too Utopian? In practice, as we have noted, by comparison with the printed word good television is usually expensive. It needs a lot of money up front, to buy film, to hire studios and facilities, to engage technicians and so on. On a national level the new producers of the cabled future would face daunting problems in making a permanent and predictable connection with their consumers. For while a smart operator might get sound backing to sell sport or new feature films on cable channels and would be sure of a good level of response and profit, would that be the case with, say, a regular programme about the problems of the Third World or a feminist view of domestic issues in Britain? Are there enough potential viewers for serious national current affairs programmes on cable television, of either the traditional or less familiar kinds? The evidence from the United States so far is not entirely hopeful: Ted Turner's buccaneering news services notwithstanding, the major commercial successes have clearly been based firmly in entertainment, providing feature films and sport. Such factual programming as there is seems to be chiefly of an informative nature, from CNN at one end to the very local programmes for the Hispanic community in Manhattan at the other. But where will programmes of general current affairs style and content fit in? What is the market for television that is neither closely news- and information-related nor clearly of documentary-feature interest? With so much more factual television available, and with the BBC and ITV still presumably broadcasting *Panorama* and *World in Action*, there must be some doubt about the prospects for more expensive and perishable current affairs, of whatever novelty and freshness.

The first clue to the answers to these questions will come from the public reaction to some of the distinctively different programming scheduled on the new fourth channel. If good audiences are discovered for the styles, perspectives and insights that we are promised, the future may be bright for current affairs on cable. Given its financial constraints, we may expect rather more studio-based current affairs from the new channel: interviews, discussions, press conferences and so on. Here again, audience response will be a good indicator for the attraction of simpler, and certainly cheaper, factual programmes on cable. The need for low production costs in a more pluralist and competitive environment is certain, either way, to indicate more talking heads and proportionately less expensive on-the-spot current affairs reporting from the ends of the earth. *Panorama* will doubtless be with us on BBC-1 to report the sounding of the Last Trump: I doubt that there will be the funds to risk an imitation on cable television. If the British audience follows the Swedish and Belgian patterns and shows a very marked inclination to maximize the viewing of entertainment programmes, the disincentive to spend large sums on new national current affairs formats will be even greater. However cheap, however limited to studio chat and simple production, the commercial logic of cable will require enough willing viewers to cover costs.

There is, however, a particular opportunity for news and comment programmes that should not be overlooked: cable is ideal for local, informational television. Our present broadcasting system is ill-suited to supplying information and comment on anything smaller

57

than a large region. True, some of the ITV companies claim a real identity with the regions they serve—Grampian, Yorkshire, Ulster, Granada, etc.—though others, notably Central in the Midlands, seem less surely founded on what we might recognize as characteristic and clearly definable parts of the realm. In the south-east the problem is even more evident: the population of the 'locality' covered by Thames and London Weekend Television is many millions strong—the south-east region of the BBC stretches from Banbury to Dover. The result is that, in a very real sense, many parts of Britain are offered regional programmes of news, comment and information that are too thinly spread over too wide an area. Research does indicate popularity: *Good Evening, Ulster* goes into 40 per cent of its area's TV homes. But the Oxford viewer is unlikely to be excited by a row over a new housing scheme in Wolverhampton. A local election sensation in Guildford is small beer to the man in the St Albans street. Yet this is the compromise that the technical limitations of transmitter broadcasting have led us to regard as the norm. Cable offers some solutions.

Any community of more than, say, 50,000 inhabitants should be able to sustain its own local cable news programme as part of a comprehensive commercial cable service. It would, of course, be a simple affair, with little more than a shoebox studio and a mobile videotape channel. As with most electronic goods, the price of simple television equipment may be expected to fall sharply as its market grows. We have become used in Britain to the excellent engineering standards, and the concomitant high costs, of our existing broadcast television. But it need not all be to that high standard, nor certainly so expensive. From 1972 to 1976 EMI ran an experimental local service in Swindon, using an existing cable network owned by Radio Rentals. Its aims were simple (it was black-and-white, not colour), and the terms of its licence from the Home Office precluded any direct revenue earning. Although it can't be compared with a properly commercial cable undertaking, therefore, some of the figures of the operation are instructive. Swindon Viewpoint provided five hours of original programmes a week (ten hours of transmissions, including repeats). Without attempting a 'hard news' service, the company provided a wide range of local programming, a good deal of which was produced by local amateurs using its facilities. Only 35 per cent of the town's 123,000 inhabitants were cabled; just over 10,000 households were thus able to see the experimental programmes. Audience research showed that about 4,400 people watched at least one programme per week. The set-up cost of £47,000 and annual operating costs of around £50,000 must be adjusted upwards for inflation but also sharply downwards to allow for the subscription charges and advertising revenue that might have been generated but for the terms of the licence. The lessons are only tentative: more comprehensive cabling, colour rather than black-and-white, a programme mix of entertainment and information would obviously suggest higher audiences and a better prospect of commercial viability. In Swindon only a small proportion of the potential audience were in any sense regular viewers. In the New York suburbs fifty-four separate cable systems have signed up over 1 million subscribers—40 per cent of families with access to cable are willing to buy its services at about £10 per month. Clearly, expansion of scale and scope must offer the possibility that sport and films will be complemented by viable local news and current affairs programmes of reasonable quality on a proper commercial basis. There are strong signs, too, that obligations will be placed on the cable licence seekers of the future to provide a public-service element among their output.

Cheap local television of this kind might easily cover the affairs and interests of a large suburb, a small town or a more widespread country area. It could be a lively forum for local issues and politics and an outlet for local societies and organizations, and it could perform many of the functions of the old small-town American newspaper. In addition to revenue from subscriptions and advertising, a variety of other local sources could be tapped for funds—local authorities, trade unions, businessmen's associations and so on. Subsequently, the higher the level of subscription, the greater the attraction to the local advertiser, the more revenue, the better the coverage and so on. For a large section of the population, information at this properly local level, complemented by a national and international news from the BBC, ITN or wherever, would probably satisfy the greater part of the need to know. An additional benefit would be the far greater possibility of general public involvement in local television, either through 'answer-back' instant polling of audiences or, perhaps more usefully, through the involvement of non-professionals in the business of production and editorial control. We may ultimately come to see our present regional arrangements as a temporary and enforced compromise, a step along a path that leads via cable, and even by new low-powered transmitters, to much more local fragmentation and local relevance.

Some parts of Britain may, of course, be able to sustain several local channels. Cable technology allows for dozens of simultaneous programmes, and many cities may develop a whole variety of cheap new local formats. Cable in New York has spawned viable programmes for the city's ethnic minorities: why not a Black London channel, or one for the Cypriot community or for Asians in Southall? Some programming could be based on very small areas indeed or on particular interest groups or activities. A group of schools, for instance, might finance the purchase of cheap video equipment to send simple programmes by cable into the homes of its pupils. Cable could eventually be highly selective about which particular homes it serves. The only limitation to the development of local 'micro-television' will be, as ever, finance and in particular the bottom-line cost of simple video cameras and recorders.

At present, we get our national television networks absurdly cheaply. In its licence fee campaign the BBC was fond of comparing the cheapness of its programmes with other forms of entertainment—the cinema, football matches and so on. And the comparison is valid. Television in Britain is now unrealistically cheap. In the United States willing subscribers pay $20 and more a month just to watch new films on subscription television: after 1986 British viewers will have the opportunity to pay to see a BBC satellite channel. Aside from the argument about creating a two-tier viewing public, there is the question of what this market will bear. How much will the ordinary family be prepared to pay for television by subscription in addition to the present licence fee? Another £25 a year? Another £100 or more? And more specifically, how much a month would you want and expect to pay for local news programmes? Would you pay £3, the price of taking a newspaper every day? Or would you pay three or four times as much? Clearly, the answers to these questions will be fundamental to the provision of new local television of any quality. So, too, will be the attitude of potential advertisers. Cable programmes known to be watched by less than 20 per cent of a town's population may have little attraction for them: for programmes seen by over 40 per cent (the New York figure) revenue should be fairly easy to raise.

On the optimistic side, it is worth recalling how readily the money was found to fund the start of Independent Television in the mid-

1950s, before profits were in sight. Much of that stake money came from shrewd newspaper proprietors, hedging their bets against electronic competition for advertising. Perhaps the process will repeat itself as the capital backing the present ITV contractors—drawn now from almost all sections of business—shifts smartly into new opportunities either for protection or for speculation. On all new frontiers much money is gambled and a good deal lost, but experiments in new local television are certain to be tried; and however dire some of the results by comparison with the polished professionalism of the networks, many will succeed and flourish.

So far I have suggested three likely consequences of the television revolution in news and current affairs programmes: first, traditional news programmes are expensive and unlikely to be replicated; second, the outlook for national current affairs is not bright—it is not the public's favourite viewing and more television will increase the viewer's ability to avoid it; third, a rapid expansion of local programming is a more optimistic proposition, as it is the realistic level at which a new audience for information and a possible new pool of finance can be expected to meet and bear fruit. But what about the existing channels during the transition? Will their traditional news and current affairs programmes change in consequence?

It is easy to overestimate the rate at which new channels will make an impact on the public. A much quoted survey claims that the population of San Diego, America's most wired city, still looks to the major networks for 88 per cent of its viewing. But even if the process is slow and old viewing habits die hard, the landscape will have begun to undergo a fundamental change. At present, our channel controllers attempt to offer balanced packages of sport, drama, news, light entertainment, current affairs, films and documentaries. Even Channel Four, with its aim of being 'distinctly different', will attempt to cover all these categories. But what does our controller do if sport is auctioned off to cable? How does he make a balanced schedule without access to the newer feature films that are being sold by subscription?

The effect will differ between the BBC and Independent Television. It is possible that the BBC might remain the last redoubt of old-style public-service broadcasting. In America, to be sure, the rapid march of entertainment on cable has led to a parallel expansion of news and public affairs in the schedules of the existing broadcasters. Network news has increased in length, and even small urban TV stations are doubling and tripling the time that they devote to news and non-fiction features. Here the BBC will remain the only organization that—given an adequate licence fee—can be sure of maintaining a fully fledged international news-gathering machine. As it will no doubt remain a national institution, providing national information and comment at a cost deeply unattractive to the new commercial cable operators, successive Governments may well feel obliged to maintain its funding at an appropriate level to guarantee these services. And, of course, the BBC may itself play a major role on the new channels. The allocation to the Corporation of two of the five British satellite channels from 1986 so far promises little for news and current affairs, but potential cable operators may be more than willing to take parts of the BBC's traditional national factual programming to stiffen up their basic fare. The BBC might itself develop into a substantial cable operator, devising new and more flexible news and current affairs programmes to suit a more diverse and fragmented viewing public. The permutations are almost endless. Cable simply means much more television, and the BBC's future may lie in part both in the provision of a greater amount of public-service material on its existing airwaves and in feeding similar output to the cable networks.

For ITV the problem is more starkly commercial. If advertising revenues are substantially tempted away from the current network to cable and satellite, its ability to maintain present styles and levels of output, on a falling income and to smaller audiences, will be swiftly diminished. If advertisers ultimately prefer to place their money elsewhere, something will have to give, and serious factual programmes will be most at risk.

As we have noted, the more television there is, the smaller the audiences for the demanding programmes. Outside the fiats and blandishments of the IBA, how long would *World in Action* or *TV Eye* survive if their audiences plunged, say, by two-thirds? How firm would the contractors' resolve be to keep them alive as income evaporated? And even if the ITV companies take a major interest in cable, which I think is inevitable, will they maintain the present level and expensive quality of these products?

That is another worst-case analysis: a deregulated free-for-all dominated by commercial interests and the need to minimize costs and to maximize audiences. A totally free system must surely major in sport, film and entertainment and leave news and current affairs to fight hard both for funding and for the attention of the viewer. It is argued, of course, that no Government would let this happen, that the development of cable will be carefully phased and licensed, that in any event the traditional fare of the current networks is too familiar and the viewing habits of the British too conservative for the old structure to vanish overnight. Perhaps. But the ecology of broadcasting may be less stable than that. However odd and quaint the present licensed monopolies of broadcasting may seem, however stuffy and élitist the presumptions of its journalists with regard to air time and the right to fill it, the television revolution, in its freest form, seems set to offer little early hope of more, better and diverse news and current affairs on the national level. Cable and satellite television are not going to be uninvented, and however fast or slow their arrival, we shall have to accommodate their dictates, a rapid intrusion of the auction and the sliderule in valuing much of what we see. By the end of the century the availability of news and comment may be limited to remodelled versions of BBC and ITV output on the national level and to local programming on myriad cable stations. The escape from the curious duopoly of the last twenty-five years, with its maddening mixture of bureaucracy and excellence, interference and interdependence, will be refreshing and even exhilarating. It will also be unpredictable, unnerving and, to some degree, destructive of many would-be broadcasters' higher hopes and expectations.

4. Film-Maker in Wonderland

DAVID PUTTNAM

'Decline' is a word that now has a permanent place in the vocabulary of the cinema. Perhaps this is understandable. Are not the massed batallions of the American major studios faced with the disintegration of their traditional markets and all the financial losses that that undoubtedly indicates? Is it not correct that in Britain, creative values aside, the climate for film-making is exceedingly arid, even with our recent Oscar success? And does not the bottom line of the business, the level of cinema attendances, continue to fall dramatically in the UK from a peak of 1.5 billion thirty years ago to a probable level of 65 million this year?

All these things are undoubtedly true, yet to label them 'decline' is to view films through the eyes of a recent, tortured past. I have no doubt that for some what is happening will mean the end, but for many others there will be fresh beginnings and new opportunities. This is a period of transition, not atrophy, though God knows, both processes can be equally painful.

We need to grasp the nettle that the entire function and economic reality of cinemas is in the process of altering for ever in the English-speaking countries. From being the main, sometimes the only, source of return for films, cinemas are beginning to take their final step as a commercial enterprise, becoming what is in effect a promotional vehicle for films whose actual pay-off will be cable, cassette, satellite and off-air broadcasting.

What we must always bear in mind is that this shift does not represent a great sea change in the expectations of the majority of those who want to *watch* films.

My own view is that 'the blockbuster' as we know it, will not survive because it is a form that demands a budgetary level that represents simply too large a risk. But the mainstream of cinema will continue to be dramatic or 'narrative' films, and they will continue to be extremely popular. Don't take my word for it. Just look at the *Radio Times* or the *TV Times* and see how films bought for television are scheduled. Watch how films are promoted in advance on the air. Television companies are as anxious to tell the public what feature films they have bought as to reveal what new programmes they have made themselves. That is why, on the day after *Chariots of Fire* had won the Oscar for best film, the BBC announced that it had bought the British television rights, and why, a little while later, Channel Four countered with the news that it had bought *Mephisto*.

People like films just as much as they ever have. What they appear increasingly to dislike is going *out* to the cinema. They prefer to be entertained in the comfort and safety of their homes. That is the root of the change we are facing, and it must be a matter of continuing amazement to us all that this shift in public taste is occurring at the very moment when technological advances are beginning to offer us the means to cater for it. Look not for conspiracy theories; the cinema industry is too fragmented to concoct one even if it tried. The timing is an accident—and a happy one.

What does this mean, first of all, for the cinema? The intelligent and ambitious cinema owner might yet find that the decade from 1985 will represent another golden era. The total number of screens will probably shrink from about 1,500 in the UK at the moment to something under 500 at the end of the decade. But I believe that the cinemas that remain will be bigger, more comfortable and necessarily based in the larger cities, and that the promotional thrust that launches films will be concentrated in those theatres.

The number of commercial cinemas will, in the end, be determined by the voracity of the cable and satellite systems that will give the films their general audience after limited theatrical débuts. It may be that this will, in fact, result in a greater number of cinemas than I envisage. If, as I believe possible by the late 1980s, three new feature films capable of making money are released each week, it could be that we will need at least that number of first-run theatres in each major city.

Once cinemas have undergone the change from being the main source of box-office revenue to being largely promotional vehicles, we could, to our amazement, find ourselves packing people in because it will have become comparatively cheap to see the films on show. The pay-off for the enthusiast who still attends will be the truly

65

cinematic experience of seeing a film on a large screen, in darkness, with the best possible sound; and the pay-off for the industry will be a promotional fulcrum around which word of mouth will feed the interest of a mass audience of cable and satellite viewers. The return for the cinema owner will no longer be box-office receipts but his stake in the home broadcasting industry. This is one reason why it is vital that, whatever decisions are made on cable, existing exhibitors and even, possibly, distributors are given the chance to participate actively.

For an analogy of what will happen when the economic balance finally tips irrevocably in the direction that I have indicated, we need to turn to the music industry. In the 1950s someone like Cliff Richard earned a fair amount of his income, probably at least half, from touring. He would set out on a sixteen-week tour of one-night stands, and commercial relationships would be established with local halls that were similar to those that exist at present between cinema owners and distributors. There was a split at the gate, money off the top and someone got the cash from the beer.

A decade later touring became a very marginal exercise, and for that reason a lot of artists did not go out on the road for a long while. There was no money in it, and bands were happy enough with the return they were making out of record sales. Then came the era of the 'super-groups'; touring again became an essential exercise to pre-sell what was now a vast number of albums. The tour itself could be a catastrophic loss-leader—the question was no longer *whether* you lost but *how much*—it was all done to sell the album, in most cases very profitably.

The day that happened, the company that owned and was booking the hall was no longer talking about how big the audience was. It was looking at the 'deal' in a totally different context. The album was the source of revenue, and the live performance a promotional exercise. Just the same sort of thing will happen with film, perhaps even to the extent that distributors will allow audiences into cinemas for free during the increasingly short period before the title is put through the 'general release' of a showing on pay-satellite or cable. This will create an entirely new commercial reality for the film industry.

As an aside and, I hope, a point of contention, it is worth mentioning that I have never understood why it is necessary to assume that going out to the cinema *has* to be substantially more expensive than sitting at home and watching the same film on your own television set. When you watch something at home, you see a smaller image, probably pre-sold, but in the comfort of your living-room, on your terms, in a manner you have chosen. When you go out to the cinema, you watch a film on my terms, on my patch, in the way that I had in mind when I became involved in producing it. There is no reason why what is essentially a qualitative decision should continue to be cost-related, as it has been up to now, largely for historical and technological reasons.

It is sometimes said that this transference from the public location of the cinema to the privacy of a suitably equipped front room is socially regressive. I do not feel competent to argue that case, nor even to counter the other popular contention, that any move from our current system of cheap television to 'paid-for' (cable) television is equally regressive, if not positively devisive and elitist. Perhaps it is, but if this is true, all technology could be held to be elitist, particularly at its inception. There will always be households that do not own a telephone or a colour television set.

Such arguments are, uncomfortably, typical of many that we have seen emerge from within the television industry. These tend to obscure the fact that our existing television system cannot, in the long run, sustain its present pattern of development, with or without competition from other systems. I feel sure that the future will reveal that many of the staunchest defenders of the 'public-utility' notion of television have also been aggressively grinding their axes during the course of the debate, using their potent moral position to obscure their more complex objectives.

The equivalent arguments, when marshalled in the context of cinema, tend to be allied to a romantic view of the future. I would prefer that we came to terms with the fact that film and television technology is now racing ahead of the creative forces that ought to guide it. We need to address ourselves to the changes that are likely to come about and to temper our aims accordingly.

Clearly, there are still many vital decisions that must be made before we can hope to see the relationship between television and film stabilized in a way that will suit both. At the moment it is one-sided and very much in favour of the networks: BBC and ITV show about fifteen hours of films a week and pay about £15 million a year for the privilege. There is no direct conduit by which that money can be recycled into new production, and very little makes the journey by a more circuitous route. Inexplicably, the Eady levy,

67

effectively a tax on cinema seats, does not apply to TV showings.

This is just one anomaly in an unsatisfactory system. If one accepts the underlying rationale of the Eady levy system, it is self-evident that television ought to be contributing as much to the fund as the cinema. In addition I would contend that Eady points us forward in one significant direction. It represents a levy on profits that remains outside the Exchequer and is redistributed, through the subventions, back into the industry, supporting the National Film Finance Corporation, the National Film School and other industry-related commitments. That sort of mechanism can work, and it could be used as the blueprint for a levy on cable profits. Simply to privatize the cable system without instituting such a mechanism for recycling profits for the benefit of the industry would be the greatest folly.

Some interesting and impressive attempts at film production have been made by ITV companies, and they should be encouraged to move further in this direction. An important step would be to amend the existing legislation that precludes the off-setting of equity investment in films by ITV companies against their payments of the Exchequer levy. Such an amendment has been continually urged by the Government's Interim Action Committee and other industry bodies. If this were done, a significant proportion of the ITV systems' buying power could be channelled into encouraging domestic production of a quality more consistent with the needs of a British audience and the ambitions of an international one. On the assumption that the ITV companies choose projects well, the loss to the Exchequer would be more than compensated for by the income that would be received from the film projects.

This would hasten us further towards the inevitable blurring of the increasingly unnecessary distinction between cinema and television. The barriers that exist —from the reluctant nervousness of the trade unions to its mirror image at the Exchequer—only serve to delay our acclimatization to a process that technology and public taste is ineluctably bringing down upon our heads.

For the British film-maker, relationships with existing television companies are fundamental, and none more so than those with Channel Four. It is not yet sufficiently widely appreciated outside the industry just how new and valuable this concept is. For the first time, independents have a mass-audience outlet capable of commissioning and financing work from a wide range of creative sources. The budgets that Channel Four's finances dictate may not be overwhelming—and this, initially, will be no bad thing—but the breadth of opportunity and originality of approach can only stimulate film-makers. And by investing in films that will have the potential of both cinema and television showings, Channel Four points the way ahead.

But the most important source of production finance will eventually come not from the conventional networks but from the pay-as-you-watch cable and satellite systems that will rise to challenge them. It is no exaggeration to say that the shape and ownership of these systems will decide whether the benefits of this burgeoning of output will go to British film-makers or to the American studios, who already have the advantages of adequate financial resources, a broad technological base and sophisticated international marketing experience.

Home Box Office in America has already proved that there is a market for a channel devoted to new films. There is every reason to suppose that here the demand is as great, perhaps even more avaricious. The three-year ban on the television showing of new films would not apply to cable, so titles would have the potency of new releases. Surveys of video cassette recorders in the UK have already shown that films are among the most popular items to be taped from television.

The fledgling subscription schemes that we already have seem to indicate that viewers are willing to pay £100 a year for a film channel. On this flimsy basis, calculations are now being made that suggest that a cable/satellite network with 2 million subscribers grossing £200 million (equal to the combined budgets of BBC-2 and Channel Four) is on the cards.

This is probably a gross underestimate. In particular, once cable systems are established and expand beyond the basic area of feature films, the fees paid for such services will rise, in present-day terms, to a figure approaching £500 per annum for each working household, and this well before the end of the century. We have enough examples before us to know that if the technology matches itself to public taste, mass use well beyond 2 million households is likely.

Existing television networks should not rest easy that the size of the subscription market will remain so modest. Nor should they expect that the cream of popular broadcasting, whether it be films or sport, will for ever remain their God-given right. Perhaps instead of looking for perpetual rights to the Cup Final, they should divert their energies to seeking out some new and vigorous role for the future.

There have been so many predictions about what the eventual level of cable subscription will be and how much subscribers will eventually be prepared to pay for a sophisticated service that they have sometimes obscured a more subtle and important point. This is that the nature of the cable service will, to a large extent, dictate its content.

Let me suggest one possible development. A national cable network is created on an area-by-area basis. Franchises are awarded to companies to provide the cable service; existing exhibitors are given an option to join the franchise companies. These companies are served by specialist programme distributors, a business in which film distribution companies find that they have a natural interest. These new distributors could become important sources of production finance.

In awarding the franchises, the licensing authority demands to know about the applicant cable companies' plans for financing British production, either through their own resources or through those of their suppliers, and gives preference to those companies that guarantee to bring new capital—as distinct from existing production capital—into domestic play.

Let us consider another option. The franchises are awarded to reputable companies that maintain that they wish to provide a mass subscription service and are unfettered by serious restrictions to their content. When the service arrives, the maximum number of hours are filled with low-cost reruns supported by the occasional new product to justify the subscription fee. The franchise company is well placed to make very high profits, few of which will return to British films.

Both hypotheses are perfectly plausible. The last obstacle to either is technology, and within a year, when the Government has made up its mind about the shape of cable, we shall know one way or the other. In my view, the second of these alternatives must be held, by contemporary standards, to be unacceptable.

Whatever happens, we can look to a future 'pay-per-view' scenario in which perhaps three new dramatic feature films will be released each week, from diverse sources. Of those, let us assume that one will be very successful and that a few of the major hits will be so popular that they will become perennials, played and replayed over the years. What film-makers will have to seek is conditions in which the majority of those films *at least break even* as a sane alternative to the present (non) economics that assumes a multitude of catastrophic losses will be paid for by one runaway success. Equally, I would like to see a situation in which even the super-hits do not return vast profits *in cash* but rather provide a form of credit that gurantees their makers a future level of production activity. The cash payment of super-profits would inevitably promote a return to the self-destructive cycle of the system. We would then be involved immediately with mega-buck directors and mega-buck stars, and the industry would corrode in the way that has become all too familiar to us.

I do not imagine that budgets will, on present terms, move much beyond the $3 million to $10 million range. One way in which they could be held at that level would be to allow technological advances in film-making to be exploited to the full, permitting a reduction in schedule lengths and, to some extent, manning requirements.

From the audience's point of view, the medium will become more intimate. Even though television sets will become larger, they will not require the scale of image that the cinema screen demands. This may offend purists who believe that the framing of an image for the cinema is necessarily grander than that of a scene destined for television. But on the sort of budgets we are talking about we will find that film-making on the grand scale is a thing of the past. Furthermore, it is only by historical accident that television screens are square; I would not be at all surprised if the new generation of television screens changes in shape.

If there will not be a place for a director working on the scale, of, say, David Lean, there will be more scope for the Ingmar Bergman or Ken Loach breed of film-maker. So films will not necessarily become trivialized. Efforts like the British Film Institute's regional theatres will become a more and more potent and important part of the cultural mix. But we must not be fooled into believing that a romantic image of the cinema—which, incidentally, I share, to my cost—can or must be maintained in the face of economic reality. The BFI's role as the cultural guardian of cinema as we know it should in many ways become easier as its brief becomes more clearly defined. This is one of the many areas that should receive an adequate level of subsidy from the cable system.

As far as so-called 'art' movies are concerned, I expect to see an increase in the number of releases. The falling-off will occur among

71

the blockbusters. People like Steven Spielberg and George Lucas will be able to survive very happily to the end of this century by adopting a kind of Disney approach. They will make their own films, find their own means of distribution and remain outside the core of the business, selling each film on the strength of the name of its maker and the promise that it will be a certain type of product, meeting specific expectations.

We need to direct ourselves to the future of the next generation of film-makers. On my estimates, they will be encouraged to produce some 150 English-language films a year, whereas in 1982/3 we will be lucky to see half that number emerging from the traditional sector. In time this evolutionary process will be transferred to other markets, foreign-language outlets and the Third World. It will all hang on the question of technology and, in the case of the West, conflicting backgrounds.

Television and cinema have evolved separately and differently; soon, not many miles down different roads, they *must* find a way to converge. Future film directors will be grounded in television and film finance will move in the same direction. Yet we are saddled, inadvertently, with anomalies that stand in our way. That is one reason why Channel Four is so important—it could help to bring to an end a ridiculous situation in which freelance film-makers have effectively been prohibited from working in television.

Throw into this mix peripheral but important issues such as the video cassette market, and you realize that we have evolved to a point at which there is a sad lack of logic and common sense in the way both film and television are ordered. The most tragic consequence of the fact that some 70 per cent of all revenue from sales of video cassettes is accruing to what is in effect a 'black market' is not that 'valuable copyrights are being infringed' but rather that much of the money that the public pays to see films on cassette is not being recycled into the production system itself. This tight cycle of production finance is too poor to be able to afford leaks. That is a lesson the Government might digest before considering throwing the cable networks open to companies that can be shown to have a less than firm commitment to production.

It must be obvious to any clear-sighted person that the gulf that is now generally perceived to exist between film and television is a nonsense. For a number of years many of us in the film industry argued for the creation of a British Film Authority to pursue the goal of rationalization. Our conviction that such a body was necessary was firm and well-intentioned. The cinema industry is too fragmented to hold dear anything but a semblance of a consensus on any important issue. It hates being told what to do. There was every reason to believe that the only way forward was through the creation of an unrepresentative body that would force a synthesis of opinion upon the industry and enable the cinema to speak with one strong voice.

I say that this *was* the case because the moment for the formation of a British Film Authority is now probably past. Had it come into being three years ago, I would have welcomed and supported its central role in fighting for the future of British cinema. Today, for all the reasons outlined here, it would be an anachronism. What the Government must create is something far more challenging, an authority to supervise the growth of the full range of visual media, both present and future. It may seem like heresy at the moment to suggest that the roles of the BBC and the Independent Broadcasting Authority are becoming obsolete, but in a very short time this will, I believe, become a fairly widely held view. It is crucial that decisions be taken before they suffer the attrition of cable, in the case of ITV through the diminution of audience levels and its consequent effect on the market, and in the case of the BBC through the impossibility of maintaining the ludicrous mechanism of the licence fee and the consequent uneasy and unnatural relationship with central government. At the same time, we will have to learn that the visual media can be viewed only as a whole, that decisions about the nature of ITV will directly affect the health of the feature film sector and vice versa.

There is something so obvious about all this that it seems bizarre that we are not yet headed down this road. The monoliths that must tumble along the way are powerful and entrenched, but in the long run it is simply a question of whether they are dismantled by design or demolished by the unstoppable force of economic reality when allied to changes in the public's taste and expectations. The cinema will shake itself out, partly through the working of market forces, but how much more sensible it would be if this transition were planned in accordance with a well thought out design instead of a throw-away doodle.

As a commercial film-maker, I am in no doubt that the single most important act in securing the future will be to recast the role of theatrical exhibition as a promotional effort in tandem with a pay-per-view cable network. Once that concept becomes clear, the rest falls into place. It begins to attack the horrendous problem of spiralling promotional costs. *Midnight Express* cost $3 million, and $7 million were spent in America alone on promoting it. That represents a general drift whose implications have taken a long time to sink in—when I came into the business, less than fifteen years ago, you simply allocated 10 per cent of the cost of the film to promotion. Now we have reached the point at which the reverse percentages are acceptable in theatrical marketing. The new technologies offer us a way through the economic jungle surrounding film production that would have seemed impossible a decade ago.

There are serious implications for the financing of features. One of the most pressing problems of the British film industry has been its depressingly small capital base, which has forced producers to go to the US majors for distribution guarantees. Cable offers new finance and will soon be a more ready source of investment than the more conventional, if uncertain, sale of theatrical rights. It also raises the point that it is becoming increasingly difficult to identify just what constitutes a feature film.

My own company, Enigma, has a deal with America's Home Box Office to make a film for which they are putting up over $2 million for the US cable rights alone. If that film proves to be a satisfactory enterprise to both of us, we also have the rights, under certain conditions, to put it out theatrically. We are making other films for Channel Four on 35-millimetre film. We took that gamble because we believe, together with our financing partner, Goldcrest, that there are markets in the world that may want these films for cinemas. But how do you describe these products—are they feature films, made-for-TV films or what?

The film industry could use cable as an opportunity to get off the reactive slide that has threatened us for the past decade. At each turn we have sought survival in the latest tax concessions or some new form of pre-sale. With this sort of guaranteed market, we could organize ourselves in a homogenous way and start to plan production. We could turn ourselves into a creative force that is not, at last, based upon greed, is not forced to make decisions out of expediency, and is free of first-past-the-post commercial competitiveness.

This would also create a challenging situation for those trade unions that are most intimately involved. Old and easy assumptions would have to be radically rethought. The entire scale of fees and residuals is, at present, based on the notion that theatrical exhibition and off-air broadcasting represents the core of income to which production activity is related. Once this ceases to be the case, each and every agreement will require a new conceptual approach to negotiation; without doubt, this will prove to be a tortuous process for everyone involved.

I hope that this will not prove to be the stumbling block that prevents British film and television production from taking full advantage of the international opportunities that will temporarily be available to it. Other countries will not be slow to exploit our hesitation and the nature of advanced technologies will make it difficult to recapture lost ground if a free-for-all eventually develops. There is a certain lack of faith within the industry that is mirrored by the attitude of the Government. Only the technological investors race ahead, perhaps oblivious to the gulf that they have created between themselves and the production sector.

In the City film finance is still regarded as a massive gamble. The fall of Lord Grade's Associated Communications Corporation has hardened entrenched attitudes. I find myself with little or no sympathy for those large investors or institutions that have found themselves caught up in a variety of well publicized film and television débâcles. The City has for years dabbled in show-business ventures—seldom have these been serious, well thought out investments. Flamboyant figures like Lord Grade are what the men in dark suits want, and the entrepreneurs merely act accordingly. Alexander Korda's maxim was 'Make your banker feel like your star, and your star like your banker.' The same principle has been applied during the past few years, with equal (fleeting) success.

I would not for one moment suggest that any investor, large or small, should put money into the commercial film industry out of altruism. What is apparent to those who look into the situation closely is that the risks associated with film can now be reduced to much more reasonable proportions, largely through pre-selling to American cable networks like Home Box Office. The intelligent investor will not be slow to recognize the spectacular opportunities that will arise in the UK as our cable market becomes a reality.

The next decade will be a roller-coaster for film makers, with all the risks and excitement that that implies. I can only hope that the end of the division between film and television will serve to bring the realm of cinema entertainment closer to economic reality. At the same time, we must make absolutely sure that public-service broadcasting and those other institutions that contribute to our country's cultural output have access to the cable revenues that technology will release. I have no interest in supporting the creation of a new generation of media moguls, be they power-mad bureaucrats, faceless chairmen or voracious entrepreneurs. I want an industry in which the average well made film, with reasonable success, offers an attractive return on investment. That will require discipline, which the cinema can and will learn from television. At the same time, television, through a closer relationship with the hurly-burly of the cinema industry, will do well to develop the necessary entrepreneurial skills that will be required if film-makers of all types are to be allowed to compete and survive in what is, whether we like it or not, an international industry. As I have said, we will learn from each other, if only because we have to.

5. *Video Education*

ROBERT ROWLAND

Perhaps it was Lord Reith's fault. The memory of his lofty asceticism was and is enshrined in that balanced trinity of purposes for a public service broadcasting organization—to entertain, to educate and to inform. The Reithian trinity, though, took on some of the patina of the man and of his times. His principles sounded fine but just a little paternal by the side of the more aggressive and more overtly jolly spirit of the new age that dawned with the arrival of commercial television and commercial radio. Even so, two of the Reithian elements were swept happily along on the new tide. Competition in information and entertainment became part of the accepted game of broadcasting.

The BBC continued to proclaim its belief in its underpinning aims, and commercial broadcasting, established as a quasi-public service body, proclaimed similar beliefs. But all such proclamations were for solemn moments, for the renewal of contracts, for the renewal of charters, for a sense of being on the side of the angels. And education became the focus of purity, rather like a middle-aged, teetotal uncle who appears every Christmas to dampen the proceedings—not unfriendly, but just a little irritating and rather dull: a family duty rather than a family pleasure. This perspective, I believe, describes much of the life and times of educational broadcasting over the last twenty-five years. And, given that the perspective has been a function of the nature of the last twenty-five years and not an act of gratuitous philistinism, it is entirely understandable.

But, of course, it is not as simple as that. Perhaps the educationalists themselves contribute to the perspective. The general audience broadcasters believe (often very reasonably) that much of what is produced is immensely educative and much more widely based than the educators can ever be. Great institutions such as the

BBC and the IBA can argue, with force, that many strands of television broadcasting combine all three of the Reithian objectives. Unlike the entertainers and the informer, the educators probably talk more about the Reithian purpose than most. Some tend to buckle it on like rusty armour to fend off the slings and arrows of diminishing air time, slender resources and what they see as a professionally unregarded product. Like Falstaff, they have been known, to overplay the force of the attack to make the armour seem stronger and the defence more virile.

From within educational broadcasting, odd paradoxes are glimpsed. Next to love and good health, it is hard to find a broadcasting colleague who does not rate education very highly in the life of his family—and, indeed, in his own life. The corridors of influence rustle with the movement of people who are actually rather proud at having done well at school or at university or, equally, find themselves distinguished for having triumphed in the face of the disadvantage of not having done well. A developed sense of culture is certainly not a drawback in the BBC.

What is it about television that has led so many to fear being seen as overtly didactic in the full glare of audience potential? Why has education become an act to be committed in the twilight? Why do even some of the educators seek to obscure their purpose and pretend that, after all, education is only like everything else? Perhaps it has something to do with that wretched Shavian aphorism: 'He who can, does. He who cannot, teaches.'

Back in the days when Shaw's reputation was climbing to its zenith, the visionaries of etherial communication were placing education at the forefront of the purposes of the new invention. Before Reith, David Sarnoff, who became President of NBC in America wrote in 1922: 'Broadcasting represents a job of entertaining, informing and educating the nation, and should therefore be distinctly regarded as a public service.' As far back as 1927 the BBC's *Radio Times* was floating the notion of a 'university of the air'. Lord Reith, in 1923, defined entertainment, through its close association with enjoyment, as

> part of a systematic and sustained endeavour to recreate, to build up knowledge, experience and character, perhaps in the face of obstacles. Broadcasting enjoys the co-operation of the leaders of

that section of the community whose duty and pleasure it is to give relaxation to the rest, but it is also aided by the discoverers of the intellectual forces which are moulding humanity, who are striving to show how time may be occupied not only agreeably but well.

On such visions the first age of broadcasting was founded. A great war had been concluded; social tensions were marked; global political assumptions were changing; the great brown scar across Europe left by the fighting seemed to carve its way across attitudes, faiths, beliefs. Broadcasting never realized those hopes in many parts of the world. But in Britain the BBC did succeed in trying to live up to them and survived, strengthened, after the Second World War. Its sense of fairness and its relatively high-minded public spiritedness seemed to articulate much that the nation had been thought to stand for when it fought against Adolf Hitler.

The second age of broadcasting, in Britain at least, began with the spread of television at the beginning of the 1950s and, above all, with the arrival of commercial television in 1955. Before it started Reith said, sourly, 'Somebody once introduced smallpox, bubonic plague and the Black Death'—a violent set of virulences to set against the cosy jingles of Murraymints. But, certainly, it could be argued that the nation was stunned by the effect of commercial television, never having had it so good before.

So the second age began, with a jingle and an embrace. High-mindedness became stuffy, arrogant, misplaced. But commercial television did Schools Television first, a kind of gamesmanship and all part of that quick greasepaint that often characterizes so many of the activities of the commercial world, best encapsulated by that brilliant semantic coup of Norman Collins, when he christened the new commercial channel Independent Television.

The BBC had been in the business of Schools Radio almost since the first cat's whisker touched the first crystal. But the teachers were suspicious. Enrichment was the vogue. Programmes were to be 'memorable interruptions' to the day's routine rather than integral parts of the pattern of teaching. With the arrival of Independent Television, consultation and liaison between the BBC and Independent Television ensured that the two television services were complementary rather than competitive. In 1982, for instance, the BBC offered nineteen series of programmes for primary schools and well over thirty series for secondary schools, ranging through history, science, languages, drama, geography and world development education, and commercial television also offered a wide service.

Beyond its provision for pupils in schools, the BBC initiated several 'further education' series in October 1962, and in 1965 a separate Further Education Television Department was formed. The Pilkington Committee of 1962 had given the initial thrust to this development with the publication of a subsequent Government White Paper, which, on the extension of television hours, said 'Educational television programmes for adults are programmes (other than Schools Broadcasts) arranged in series and planned in consultation with appropriate educational bodies to help viewers towards a progressive mastery or understanding of some skill or body of knowledge.' Perhaps the most notable achievement of this area of broadcasting has been the Adult Literacy Campaign (1975–80). This attempted to reach out to the estimated 2 million adult people with a reading age of 7 or less, and it involved close co-operation between the Government (through the Adult Literacy Resource Agency), the BBC and the local education authorities. Short TV programmes in prime time on BBC-1 were designed to encourage the non-reader to seek help. Some longer programmes were associated with work books and audio-visual materials. And at the crucial and broad base of the co-operation was a large volunteer referral service (37,000 people) to help inquirers with appropriate teaching. Broadcasting played a crucial role but a relatively slight teaching role. This creative act of multi-media partnership resulted in 200,000 people registering as students—an impressive figure by any standard.

In that post-Pilkington period, and following the birth of 'Further Education' for adults on television, there were dreams and ideas that eventually took shape in the third great development of educational broadcasting—the partnership between the BBC and the newly created Open University in 1969. In 1965 Jennie Lee, Harold Wilson's new Minister of State, building on earlier discussions between the BBC and the Government about a Correspondence School of the Air, made it clear that she was determined to have not a school but a new kind of university—'and nothing but a University'. It was to be, in her eyes, 'a university of the second chance, but not of the second best'. Her working party produced a White Paper in 1966, and the University of the Air was officially recommended. Eventually, under the leadership of the Director General, Sir Hugh

Greene, the BBC agreed to provide thirty hours of network television time and thirty hours of radio time per week to this fledgling creation—a remarkable act of vision, commitment and courage. However, the programmes, from the start, could never be designed to appeal to a large audience; and, worse, the existence of a university of the air waves might give a forbidding character to the channel. It could only be justified by being an act of public service and by representing a concern to explore the potentiality of broadcast television beyond the wider purposes that had become its stock in trade since the Coronation and the arrival of the commercial network. In its way, the founding of the Open University in 1969 was a first step towards the third age of television that is heralded so clearly now by the arrival of new delivery systems and proliferating technology in the home.

The Open University doubled the BBC's education output on television and radio, and it introduced some entirely new methods and assumptions. It was the first 'partnership' between a major broadcasting authority and an outside, independent body. The BBC and the Open University are formally related by a legal partnership agreement under the terms of which the full independence of both bodies is maintained—neither is 'in charge' of the other. The BBC's side of the partnership is paid for by the Department of Education, as part of the University's overall allocation of capital and recurrent funds. The marriage works well, with relatively few family squabbles. There are continuing anxieties, on the BBC side, that the Open University dominates too much air time, and Sir Hugh Greene's vision has not been shared by all the most senior staff who succeeded his era—though there have been one or two notable exceptions. It is certainly felt, quite strongly, that it is a little dotty to broadcast to a very small number of students (the Open University student population is around 90,000—immense by University standards, but tiny when set against the lowest expectations of a national channel). On the other side there is anxiety that the programmes are too expensive and that the constraints of airtime mean that not enough students can watch them. But the partnership survives. Well over 3,000 television programmes and 3,000 radio programmes across seven broad production or faculty areas have been made and transmitted with few serious arguments, though one institution, the Open University, is a democracy based on academic freedom and the other, the

81

BBC, is a hierarchy based on public responsibility.

Just as the birth of 'access' television in the 1970s represented an act of 'giving', so the BBC's partnership is an act of 'sharing'—and it is, conceivably, harder to share than to give. But, in my view, 'sharing' will be a growing phenomenon of the coming decade, and the educational broadcaster will find more and more partnerships and connections being forged—for financial reasons, sometimes, but, above all, for educational reasons. I believe that the work of the BBC with the Open University can stand as a blueprint and a model for those creative acts of sharing that will develop as the possibilities of the true multi-media age begin to emerge. For the academics, also, it has meant changes. The fact of broadcasting precise messages takes teaching out of the privacy of the tutorial or the lecture theatre and imposes, thereby, constraints on the concept of academic freedom. As the first Vice Chancellor, Sir Walter (later Lord) Perry, said in 1976:

> Total academic freedom on the part of all Open University staff could lead to use being made of the teaching programmes to indulge in polemic, enabling an individual member of staff to preach disaffection or even sedition to a very large audience. In the second phase, when institutional control is imposed on the content of courses, the institutions could use this power of control for propaganda purposes. It is therefore essential, in my view, to the survival of an institution of the nature of the Open University to recognize that its freedom to teach precisely what it wishes cannot be total.

New partnerships, for the use of television, therefore, do not involve an adjustment of the perspectives of the broadcaster alone.

The Open University and other aspects of educational broadcasting are fine examples of what has begun to be called 'narrowcasting', a pejorative word that is calculated to suggest diminishment by comparison with broadcasting. I prefer the concept of 'targetting' or 'aimcasting' ('narrowcasting' should be left as a definition of those programmes that only engage a tiny part of the brain). It is certainly a difficult task to produce programmes to a very precise teaching requirement, and in its Open University programmes the BBC has led the way in using the airwaves to reach very precise numbers. But the fact that the programmes are broadcast means that they also represent a rich national teaching resource and articulate a wider meaning of the word 'open'. They also allow for fresh appreciation of the nature of audiences. It has always seemed to me reasonable that serious educational material should be broadcast on the fringes of prime time. The Open University student, for instance, also wishes to see the fine play, the great event, the crucial political debate, the pop concert, the sporting schedules—and programmes with mass appeal should be transmitted, by definition, at the time of maximum mass availability. The educational broadcasters have always been anxious about being put in a 'ghetto'—as if not to be performing at prime time represented, in some curious way, the emasculation of the psyche. Hence, I suspect, some of the cries for stealth that are issued even by those with a remit to fashion the future. One of the new senior commissioning editors for the new fourth channel was quoted recently as saying of the proposed educational output on the channel: 'We will want to have our programmes all over the place, in a way that is indistinguishable from the general output and in which people don't even necessarily notice that some things are educational and some are not.' This sounds to me very like the usual old business of seeking to apologize for the word 'education'—a curious national disease. I find it hard to imagine any sports producer pretending that the Cup Final wasn't football or an opera producer seeking to jazz up *Parsifal*. I believe that educational broadcasting should be clear and confident about its purpose. It should not be afraid to be didactic. It should aspire to the highest professional standards. It should never be dull. It should seek to be different. There is an inexorable law in television that everything slowly begins to look the same. The educational broadcaster should proclaim a different purpose—for school curricula, for university students, for language acquisition, for literacy, for numeracy, for social skills, for training—and be clear about the level that is being aimed at. And not in a 'ghetto' but in legitimate educational territory on the networks. It is difficult to learn anything without working, and the educational broadcaster should not be afraid to expect the audience to work while watching. The fact that the first two ages of broadcasting have, broadly speaking, been dominated by the idea that broadcasting is for leisure and entertainment should not be a continuing prescription for the future as the function of the screen faces proliferation and change.

Internationally speaking, the change to watch is what Katz and Wedell, in their illuminating book *Broadcasting in the Third World*, have called 'extensive' as opposed to 'intensive' educational broadcasting. As the Western world faces what it believes are more and more social problems, television can play a role in helping people to overcome disadvantages, to recognize opportunities, to share concerns, to know what to consume and how to consume it. I attended a European Broadcasting Union Conference recently and watched programmes from the whole of Western Europe. Without exception, the educational broadcasters showed great concern in their programmes on how to be old, how to be a parent, how to be a voter, how to be a ratepayer, how to be a trade unionist, how to be a consumer. Throughout Europe there are needs that are not serviced by the formal educational system in any way—those of adults wishing to re-train or facing redundancy and of families with no wage-earners or on the move, those of people facing isolation and loneliness, those of the vast 'Fourth World proletariat' of about 8 million migrant and immigrant workers, those of the illiterate (in 1971, of the population over 15 at the time, there were 29 per cent illiterate in Portugal, 15 per cent in Greece, 10 per cent in Spain). Many vital efforts to help are being made in these areas, some broadcast-led and -based, some very basic and almost aggressively 'non-professional'.

Interwoven with some of the declared aims and objectives of such splendid examples as the UK Adult Literacy Campaign and Tele-Promotion Rurale in Grenoble (a multi-media system for the training of small farmers and agriculturalists), there are some interesting manipulative attitudes, expressed in such ventures as the Charleroi Collective Action project in Belgium, which proclaims itself a pilot project for a regional Open University.

> Its aim to democratize education [says a summary of its objectives] is linked to a well-founded belief that this is not possible without a democratization of society. In the learning groups, an overriding aim is to help people realize how society might be transformed in a way compatible with this all-important goal. Hence the stress on developing outcomes which, at a local level at least, might lead to the necessary understanding of social mechanisms to be able to bring about concrete changes in the community through collective action on social and economic problems.

So far, the Charleroi experiment has not used television because it has started on a grass-roots basis. Its plans for using the mass media 'are conceived within the objectives of the overall collective community action programme'. That programme provides short courses in subjects identified by target-group members as representing subjective needs (electrical wiring, health, yoga, car mechanics, photography), basic education courses (literacy, numeracy, social studies, economic and political analysis), training linked to specific projects 'of use and relevance to the community'.

In the Charleroi scheme, as in some other European schemes of local, potentially cable-based teaching, there is a deep suspicion of 'professionalism'. Educational publications are littered with references to the need to reduce the role of the professional producer, to decentralize and to lower the cost of production. In the case of the Grenoble agricultural venture the move from broadcasting to video cassette has been accompanied by a diminished role for producers and technicians. It is certainly the case that the professional broadcast media are not adept at providing material for a wide variety of intellectual attainments; the length of programmes is finite, the pace non-personal. How to reconcile a wide variety of learner needs and motivations with the economies of scale proper to centrally organized projects operating at national and regional levels is a key question.

In China, Pakistan, Latin America, Africa, the Middle East, television is playing an increasingly important role in education. Over thirty refinements of the British Open University system are being studied or implemented. The attractions of integrated distance-teaching are many: it is relatively cheap; it obviates the need for a concentration of students on campus; it enables a very small number of skilled teachers to be used to maximum effect (and there is a desperate shortage of teachers in the world). But the early emphasis on central provision is being affected by concepts of access and participation, together with those thrusts of social concern that, in some eyes, appear to confuse the educator's role with that of the old priesthood. A recent World Bank study stated that 'educators now see education less as a distinct sector than as part of the overall development process, whether this be social or individual.' The role of television is building on the long and continuing tradition of radio in the Third World: radio schools in Latin America, farm forums in India, Tanzania, Ghana. The McBride Commission defined the function of the media in the less developed countries ambitiously: 'Communication should be considered as a major development resource, a vehicle to ensure real political participation in decision-making, a central instrument for creating awareness of national priorities.' It all feels a long way from those 'memorable interruptions' to the day's routine offered by BBC Schools radio in the 1920s. But it is possible, of course, that the McBride report overstated the potentialities of the media. Certainly, the line between a proper ambition to explore the educational purposes of the medium and hubris is sometimes quite thin.

Television is, arguably, the most powerful form of communication that has been invented since print. There is a great fear in the non-Western world that it will be abused, that material from different cultures will be imported that could help to fracture local beliefs, attitudes, harmonies. There is a growing realization that the dangers of cultural domination are intense, as the sharp imperatives of commercialism bring Western soap operas, serials, assumptions, in to the homes of Djakarta, Lagos and Caracas. Side by side with this anxiety is a real desire to use the medium to address some of the enormous problems faced by people in those parts of the world that share the sun with the West but precious little else.

At independence, in 1948, Pakistan, with a population of 30 million people, had about 17 million illiterates over the age of 9. In 1981, with a population of about 84 million, she had an illiterate population of 45 million. Hence a drive to teach the illiterate through television. A similar question of scale underlies the development of the Chinese Central Broadcasting and Television University, which is the focal point for twenty-eight local broadcasting and television universities. The intake of students in 1979 and 1980 was 417,000. The university has three hours' morning and three hours' afternoon air time, six days a week, on the nationwide TV channel. The television schedules put entertainment aside, and a recent visitor said: 'with this pervading desire for learning and the determination to pursue it at all times and places, allied with the structure and means to deliver at a distance, China appears to be on the brink of a great breakthrough in universal education.'

In India the satellite has been enlisted in the service of education. Television began in India only as recently as 1959, when a small 'experimental' station was set up in Delhi. Its original objectives were educational and developmental, and television sets were installed in community centres and in schools. But the programme content underwent a steady change, and within a few years the bulk of transmission time was being devoted to entertainment, to what is called 'general programming'. But the educators hung on, and eventually their persistence led to the India–USA Satellite Instructional Television Experiment (SITE) in 1975, a pioneering exercise in the use of direct satellite broadcasting for educators. It involved the transmission of four hours of television programmes every day to 2,500 remote villages; the basic instructional content covered the fields of family planning, health, agriculture and teacher training. The experiment was closely monitored. The villagers had never seen television before, and after their early curiosity wore off, the first month's average evening audience of 300 settled down at about 100 per set. With the intention of reducing programming costs, an attempt was made to dub two sound tracks on to a single programme beamed at paired neighbouring states that spoke different languages (Andhra Pradesh and Karnataka in south India, for example). This event has been described as probably the largest communication experiment of modern times.

Experiments abound right across the world. Open Universities are being considered and opened from Venezuela to Thailand. Studios and high technology pour into places where nomads walked only a few decades ago. The proliferation of method and ambition is dazzling—and everywhere educational ambitions have to fight for time as the tidal wave of commercialism flows through the screens of the world. This country has been at the forefront of developments in television—the first television service in the world from Alexandra Palace, the first news bulletins, the first outside broadcasts, the first schools broadcasts, the first Open University. Now the scene is changing once again.

Among the swirling counter-currents, which will emerge as the main flow? With satellites, cable, video cassettes, video discs, telephone conferencing, teletext, greater choice, will education have a lesser or a greater role to play on the screen? Will it become more or less closely related to the great professional broadcasting organizations? Will every school or university become its own video publisher? If so, who will set the standards? Will mass problems be best solved by the retreat of 'education' from the great channels? Will the channels deserve to survive if some of the strands of their rich texture are woven into different methods of delivery? Having seen technological investments gathering dust in Saudi Arabia and Venezuela for lack of skills to use them, I prefer to be cautious about the future. Some people's dreams of the role of the media have been over-ambitious and unrealized. But there are moves afoot that I believe will radically alter the role of the screen in education and the business of producing for it.

The development with, I believe, the greatest and most fascinating impact is the video cassette and, as it develops, the video disc. For the first time since its invention the moving electronic image has ceased to be ephemeral. It can now be stored, replayed, indexed: it is recoverable. For the first time print has a real rival. In its way, that is a stunning enough thought. But all will depend on the machines' penetration of the home. If they succeed, the implications for instruction and education are almost awesome. The signs are that they will. The take-up of rented video cassette machines is faster than the penetration of colour television and exceeds the industry's predictions. Over 10 per cent of homes now possess a television recording device. It took a hundred years for the telephone to reach 75 per cent of British homes. By comparison, it took twenty six years for radio to reach 75 per cent of homes, seventeen years for television, fourteen years for colour television. If VCRs continue to spread, they could reach 75 per cent of homes within ten years. It is often argued, with some force, that certain transmissions, such as Open University programmes, should move on to cassette. The University has moved massively to audio cassette over the last few years, and there will soon be a move to video cassette, bringing with it enthusiasm for exploring a new relationship with print. But as long as the networks are important delivery systems they should retain an educational brief in order to maintain their rich texture, to broaden their scope, to fulfil their function of providing, in accordance with the public-service principle, access to material that would otherwise be denied to non-formal participants in education.

I believe that video cassettes will bring more and more multi-media, closely integrated packages of material with a wide variety of purposes—the teaching of technical and personal skills, the exploration of mathematics in a wholly new way, the facilitation of scientific experiments. Both the role of the producer and the end product will change. The producer will shed the constraints of the ephemeral quality and precision of transmission time that underpin so many of the skills of the broadcaster. Non-linear programming will develop side by side with traditional programmes that are made to live in a particular space or at a particular time. It will be possible to gather and present evidence in its raw state. The links with print will be closer. The need for face-to-face support may diminish. Students will be able to decide on their own schedules. And with the capacity of off-air and time-clock recording, hours that are rejected at the moment will be available for many kinds of educational activities.

Moves in this direction have already taken place. Instructional video is in the market place. Reworkings of Continuing Education series are on offer. The Open University is now preparing courses with 'video-only' components, and these will probably command much more of the students' time than traditional television. (A video disc experiment is also in preparation, in which the text and the moving image will be recoverable on a single disc.) Ninety per cent of secondary schools now have access to a video recorder, and the recorded use of some BBC Schools TV series, has risen to over 95 per cent. The provision of units of programmes expressly designed for the purpose of recording is now well established in Schools TV; like those of the Open University, some of these units have helped to develop new television techniques.

Just as the professionals can discern among the new media new opportunities and new relationships (between print and video, between teacher and producer, between researcher and educationist), so some educators can discern the opportunity to return to privacy. It is thought by some that video cassettes could be cheaper than television programmes; with the removal of the art of transmission for these products, the need for broadcast quality will diminish, runs the argument. I believe, on the contrary, that as video cassettes for instruction and for learning begin to spread and students scrutinize them closely, replay them, study them, their quality will have to improve, technically and intellectually. I will expect a recording of the *Eroica* to be as fine as, even better than, transmission over the air.

With the arrival of satellites, other new adventures are in the offing. There is the possibility of genuine co-production, say, in Europe. As a possible model for this, first steps have been taken, under the auspices of the Council of Europe, to prepare materials for a European course for the training of adult educators in different centres in Europe. The video materials draw on the experience of various countries and are translated into different languages. Although this is a small and rather arcane step, the concept of approaching problems with a fully interactive European perspective is exciting. Problems of unemployment, problems of migration and so many of those areas of social concern that merit television attention (and not just as objects of report or inquiry) will be able to use the satellite for educational objectives. The capacity of the satellite to share experiences and material is as important as its capacity to speed communication. If and when satellite transmissions and link-ups with cable have spread far and wide (and I believe it will be quite a long time before satellite penetration of homes matches that of the video cassette or disc), more collaborations will emerge.

Equally, nations will co-operate to explore the uses of cassette and disc, possibly linked with broadcasting in a mixed economy of delivery. The spread of computer literacy and instruction in the principles and practice of the new machines will be a challenge for the video producers and the networks. The BBC's micro-computer course is an important step along this road. As old industries die and new ones (it is hoped) are created, the need for retraining will be a major job for the video producers and the networks. The Government has been exploring the possibility of an Open Technical College, less centralized than the Open University, a looser set of national and local arrangements, with video playing as important a role as broadcasting. And there is now much talk of the interactive possibilities of micro-processors linked to the television screen. Already there are micro-computer games of chess, tennis and mathematical and foreign-language instruction. Access to a large computer would, in theory, allow for a limitless range of interactive programmed instruction and learning, though I think it will be some time before such computer-based, interactive developments occur.

The drive towards cable and the potentialities of local interaction will allow the thrust of the main providers to be geared more and more to local needs and requirements. The established networks, for all the arguments, have served educational broadcasting well over the decades. The growing pressure of commercialism (and nobody could argue that education, in the precise sense, is a commercial proposition by comparison with other kinds of programming) may make it harder for them to continue to provide such a service, but I believe their responsibilities will win the day. Consequently, it is vital that new cable developments be properly regulated so that contractors' obvious financial opportunities will be complemented by a sense of responsibility to the community. A deregulated cable system, with a deregulated direct broadcasting satellite system, would be like taking an excavator to Lords. So much that has been carefully nurtured, so much that has been won and maintained, so many national responsibilities could be lost in the web of cable proliferation.

Beyond hopes for the satellite as an agent of a real international perspective and the cable as a disseminator of the perspective, with the added capacity to define issues in terms of local needs, there lie all the new devices that are emerging with their own voices about the future: teletext and printouts from the screen; a device called Cyclops that uses both tracks of a stereo sound cassette (one to supply sound and the other a picture display) to provide an effective, interactive electronic blackboard; even telephone conferencing, as in the University of Wisconsin system, which presses the first of the mass electronic inventions into the service of ear-to-ear teaching. Whatever the future holds, it is clear that television (and the sharing of sound) will undergo a serious change. It will cease to be just a provider of entertainment, enlightenment and educative enrichment (though that has been a noble enough task in its first forty-five years). It will become a show to be stopped, a face to argue with, a dexterous object. For those who could afford it, the invention of print democratized knowledge. The slow spread of literacy caught up with the invention—over a very long period of time. The invention of Marconi's universal sound was an extraordinary spur to perceptions and knowledge, aided by the new technologies of the mass press. With television, the pace got hotter and the speed of delivery and the needle thrust of the new technology (one could argue) was inimical to contemplation and the widely differing personal skills of understanding. The broadcast technology of television had to assume a mean of understanding, a mean of receipt, a mean of fascination. Thus has arisen the extraordinary, and often unquestioned, singularity of the audience concept, which sometimes obscures the fact that *Panorama* (on a good night) reaches the equivalent of fifty or sixty packed Wembley stadia. The idea that such a crowd has any homogeneity is odd at best. But in the early ages of broadcasting the technology of television delivery needed to assume such homogeneity.

The new technologies will allow for personal speed, quick and slow. Through that they will be able to build on all the work of the educators on the vast networks who have sought to uphold the claims of contemplation and the controlled acquisition of knowledge. It is my belief that the job has been well done and that, through the screen, great successes have been achieved. Languages have been introduced, social problems tackled, new technologies addressed, the shape and rhythm of mathematical equations demonstrated. The networks will retain their importance for some years to come, and the dreams of Reith and Sarnoff should still influence them. But changes in technology will bring new opportunities—and new responsibilities. The screen will be able to teach like a book or a friend. It will be able to develop all that has been achieved with a new diversification of methods—late-night transmission for recorded use, video delivered through the post, computers that provide for interaction, satellites (linked to cable and recording devices) bringing multi-lingual perspectives, discs with the capacity to present 40,000 instantly recoverable stills and limitless instantly recoverable demonstrations, thoughts, ideas, pictures.

It has always been the case that the future never comes as fast as all of us, bound to our own lifespans, would like to feel is inevitable (if only so that we can enjoy more choices and experiences). But we do all have calculators and, if we wish, digital watches. Man has stood on the Moon. Television has seized the world. Recording machines are in the home. The gramophone record has immortalized the voice of Caruso.

Just as the first age of broadcasting was heralded in Britain, the USA, India, South America by a declaration of educational intent, so the third age will bring education back into the pantheon. It is our job to make sure that it doesn't slip away. Not to be educated, not to have the confidence to be uncertain through one's knowledge, is one of the greatest disabilities that a child can suffer. The screen will help to ensure that fewer suffer from that disability. It will provide a wonderful opportunity for the broadcaster, for the educator, for the academic, for the schoolteacher. We shall all have to share our skills to make the cassettes, the discs, the satellites, the cables twinkle with a purpose beyond that of the salesman or the entertainer. For those who come to the world of education on the screen from the equally demanding world of journalism, the search for truth and understanding will be a shared objective. As has been said so often before, it is not enough just to report events: understanding should accompany rapid snapshots of a politically spinning world. And understanding, with all that that means, has to be taught. Perhaps that aphorism of Bernard Shaw, who dismissed television when it started, should be reworded: 'Those who can, should teach: those who can't shouldn't.' Then it all begins to sound like a daring, even dangerous, challenge.

6. *Paperback Television*

PAUL BONNER

Crouched in the back of a camera car on a bleak road in Smethwick in 1964, I was filming a Mr Singh, wired with a radio microphone, going into the local hairdresser's. I listened on headphones as Mr Singh was told that the shop was closed—at 11.30 a.m. on a Tuesday morning. Patiently and politely he pressed his point: 'You do cut hair, don't you?'

'Yes.'

'You are the only barber in this area?'

'Yes.'

'But you won't cut my hair?'

'No, I'm closed.'

'On a Tuesday morning?'

'Yes.'

'Are you sure you don't want to cut my hair? I will pay well for having my hair cut in your barber's shop.'

'No, I am not cutting your hair.'

'But that man in that chair is having his hair cut, and you won't cut mine?'

'No.'

'Why won't you cut it?'

Finally the hairdresser broke: 'Because you're dirty.'

Needless to say, Mr Singh was fastidious about personal hygiene. But an audience watching television at that time had no access to such information—or to information about any other significant feature of Mr Singh's culture—unless I, or someone like me, provided it. Of course, broadcasters did their best to examine and explain; we shall see that some qualities have been lost as others have been gained on the road towards equal opportunities for all to broadcast.

Mr Singh was filmed in the days long before the Broadcasting

Complaints Commission, when you didn't have to acquire several different permissions to film from a hidden camera with a radio microphone. Only the year before I had filmed, through a two-way mirror, a salesman working for John Bloom and had caught him doing his illegal switch-selling as he talked to a housewife in her kitchen. Two years after Mr Singh a well-meaning but misguided BBC producer put a radio mike in the handbag of a homeless lady going into the Housing Office of BBC TV's own local council (Hammersmith). The resulting tape, when broadcast in a current affairs magazine programme, revealed what appeared to be the stony-heartedness of a socialist council. Repercussions caused the setting up of so many regulations about the use of hidden filming that it was never again used successfully to explore the anatomy of anti-social and reactionary elements in British society.

I am sure that the ban on hidden filming is not the reason why the nature of prejudice has not been explored on television as forensically as it should have been, but the complex clearance regulations indicate an institutional attitude on the part of British television that has militated against the exploration of many situations in which man exploits man. Yet it is precisely such exploitation that many groups and individuals within our society want to see explored and revealed on television.

Moves in that direction began in the autumn of 1971 with the now famous *Late-Night Line-Up* programme in which Tom Corcoran and Eddie Montague, desperate for an item for that evening's programme, went out to the canteen of the Guinness factory in Park Royal, Acton, with a camera crew and reporter Tony Bilbow to listen to the workers' views on the week's television. They used the *Radio Times* and the *TV Times* as an agenda. As Bilbow questioned them, the great gulf that existed between those well paid and intelligent but working-class people and the broadcasters who were providing programmes for them became apparent. At some point in the programme one of the workers turned to camera and said: 'For example, you are going to edit this, and we'll turn out saying something totally different from what we really said.' The others agreed. The voice of Eddie Montague from behind the camera was heard saying, 'We'll put it out exactly as we shot it, clapper-boards and all.' To his credit, Rowan Ayres who was the editor of *Late-Night Line-Up* at the time, did just that. He ran the two rolls of film from start to finish, with no edit.

That transmission was a fascinating illustration of the gap between the broadcasters and their audience. It was not the world's most exciting programme, judged by the norms of television then or now, but it was a programme with a strangely disturbing quality. It became the example that allowed some members of the *Late-Night Line-Up* production team under Rowan Ayres and Mike Fentiman to propose that the BBC should set up a unit in which programmes could be made by outsiders, with the help of BBC staff. To the Director-General, Charles Curran, a committed seeker after an 'objective' editorial position, this was tantamount to heresy. But the Controller of BBC-2, David Attenborough, saw the merit in an experiment designed to find out what would happen if people were given their own air time on television. He pursued the idea vigorously with his Managing Director, Huw Wheldon, and the Director-General. There was sympathy for the idea on the part of some members of the BBC's Board of Governors, which approved an experimental series at a meeting in December 1972.

In the end—as happened not infrequently on *Late-Night Line-Up* (or 'Leak-Night Line-Up', as it was known in Fleet Street)—it was a word to Elkan Allan on the *Sunday Times* that led to the BBC's appearing to have publicly declared itself to be going ahead with such an experiment. This was not a promise that was easy to reverse in a climate in which the new Labour Government included a senior Minister, Tony Benn, who during the run up to the Election had made the memorable comment: 'Television is too important to be left to the broadcasters.'

Eight years before as Mr Singh came back across the road to the camera car after being thrown out of the shop by the hairdresser, I had wound down the window and said, 'That was terrific, Mr Singh.' My 'terrific' television had been his indignity. Perhaps that incident served to make me acutely aware of the gap that exists between the achievements of television and the hopes of its audience. Britain's various component communities—particularly those with coloured skins—often feel that the consensus approach of the BBC and Independent Television's news and current affairs broadcasting has little to say to them.

Yet, this has not always been so. I remember, just after the first Notting Hill riots in the mid-1950s, when BBC Television devoted an hour of peak time on its only channel to James Baldwin talking to Peter Duval Smith about the anatomy of racial prejudice. It was hailed by the black people who, before the regentrification of Lime Grove (the street) used to sit out on their front steps and call encouragement or disparagement to anyone who emerged from the Lime Grove studios, a form of audience feedback that, alas, cannot be artificially revived. There were also the early *Tonight* programmes, which carried reports by a West Indian of the way in which his people were treated as they sought housing and jobs. In the early 1960s perhaps the most objective of all explorations of the nature of the effect of colour prejudice on a family was carried by Rediffusion in a *This Week* programme made by Desmond Wilcox and Bill Morton and called *A Nigger for a Neighbour*. Furthermore, Richard Taylor, the director who worked with me on the *Human Side* colour-prejudice programme in Smethwick, went on to make the programme that first revealed the tensions that were being built up between the police and the coloured communities (it was called *Equal Before the Law* in the *Cause for Concern* series).

But despite these distinguished, pioneering antecedents, from the middle of the 1960s to the early 1970s there was a woolly liberal belief that the new, 'real' democracy attributed to Marcuse by Danny the Red, Tariq Ali and the rest had changed the world so that the ethnic communities could be embraced by a sort of 'love-in' replacement for consensus. I may be wrong, but other than Richard Taylor's *Cause for Concern*, I don't think there was a truly memorable programme that contributed to the understanding of the tensions and ambitions of ethnic minorities between 1966 and 1972. Demands built up during this period for a view of the world on television that was not dominated by consensus-seeking, grey-flannel minds, and not from ethnic communities alone.

Then suddenly a lot of things happened in a twelve-month period. Public memory recalls the Heath Government being toppled by the miners in 1974, after the three-day week. The key battle of the miners' campaign was fought at the gates of the gasworks at Saltley, in Birmingham. Predictably, television's main response was to provide its usual psephological approach to the election. It took little note of the very deep changes that were occurring in the working-class constituency groups of socialism. Yet a year earlier the BBC had started to provide half an hour of air time, late at night on BBC-2, during which all comers could state their views of the world: it was called *Open Door*.

It has become fashionable now to deride *Open Door* as a very limited form of access, and indeed it was, but in so deriding it we should not forget its extraordinary achievements in those early days. The first programme, transmitted on 2 April 1973, attracted considerable attention but was, sadly, a rather confused appearance by the St Mungo Community Trust, who had bought succour—as they still do—to at least a section of the itinerant homeless in London.

By the time the *Open Door* programmes had become more interesting, people were not watching them in great numbers any more. Less than 100,000 people saw a programme in which a group of black teachers opened up a debate about the cultural survival of blacks in an educational system devised by whites for whites. In programme number thirty-five Ed Goldwyn helped the Immigrant Workers Group to make an *Open Door* that revealed for the first time the extent of racial prejudice within Britain's Trade Union movement. I remember, too, the astonishment with which, in the autumn of 1973, I watched Angela Kilmartin groaning on the lavatory in the middle of the night—*on television*—to make a graphic plea for a better understanding by the medical profession, and by males in general, of that extremely unpleasant disease from which only women suffer called cystitis. Here were two minority groups— one of them a minority of 51 per cent—whose very real anxieties had hitherto been ignored almost totally by the vast resources of television.

By the time that Rowan Ayres left *Open Door*, after the first twelve programmes, I had spent ten years in the privileged position of being one of perhaps fifty people (0.00001 per cent of the population) who were regularly making documentaries for British broadcast television. I had thought, of course, that mine connected with my audiences' needs—don't we all? However, Mr Singh's face lingered in my mind, and some of the more realistic 1960s discussions of a fairer media world had made their impact.

So I agreed to take over from Rowan. The experience was a revelation. The process of encouraging people who had applied for air time to make programmes in their own way, and of helping them with the physical task of so doing, was a self-denying ordinance of an enormous magnitude for all the staff who worked on the programme. Most of them were what the BBC then called production assistants (now assistant producers), many of them on temporary attachment. They laboured long hours, often with groups that were suspicious of the organization that we represented and sometimes with groups who, faced with the opportunity of saying what they stood for, became divided among themselves about what it was that they did represent.

Groups and individuals often wanted to break the BBC rules of one sort or another. In the autumn of 1975 Gentle Ghost, an alternative communal work group from Notting Hill, wanted to open its programme with a full frontal male nude. He would represent, they said, primitive man emerging from the primordial surf, and he would go round the studio being steadily bowed down by the baubles of consumer society—radios, cameras and the like. When I said to the group that full frontal male nudity might cause the audience to get the wrong idea about some of the more important aspects of the group's work, I was greeted not with guffaws, which perhaps I deserved, but with the comment: 'But man, violence is a greater obscenity than nudity', a statement with which it is difficult to disagree. In the end we reached a compromise, whereby it was evident that the man was naked but, on the other hand, his appearance was not a full frontal confrontation with the audience.

In programmes on issues like race—in which whites campaigned against 'immigrants' and black youths from Kentish Town inveighed, in their own patois, against honky values in general and police brutality in particular—the institutional pressures of the BBC upon *Open Door* were not particularly forceful. In fact, by Alasdair Milne at Television Centre and by the late Desmond Taylor, who was called Editor, News and Current Affairs, we were positively encouraged to realize the ambitions of every group—within the constraints of a tight budget. This was the time of the Annan Committee, which took evidence both from the groups who had broadcast on *Open Door* and from the *Open Door* Community Programmes Unit staff. The enlightenment of the programmes did something to redeem BBC's slightly tarnished image at the beginning of the Annan investigation. It was not until Ian Trethowan became Managing Director of Television that difficulties began to arise over what each group wanted to use its air time to say and what help it might have in saying it. Even then (although CND, the Campaign against Racism in the Media and the Newcastle Centre for Unemployment would disagree), access to BBC Television could generally be said to be unfettered. And behind these occasional 'political' skirmishes, which inevitably hit the headlines, the

99

Community Programmes Unit staff were pioneering techniques for better, 'fairer', access that, equally inevitably, did not claim the attention of the press—though Peter Fiddick of the *Guardian* and Chris Dunkley of the *Financial Times* did write about our work.

I suppose the most important development in these years was 'mobile editing'. The BBC's Film Department had set up a mobile film-editing facility that was used primarily for drama, to assemble 'rushes' sequences on location so that the director of a play could see that it worked before cast and props were scattered to the four corners of new productions. The redoubtable Eddie Montague (whose broadcasting craft skill was film editing) proposed that we edit *Open Door* so that a whole group making a programme could help to put it together instead of nominating a representative to approve what we had done on its behalf, since, however careful the BBC mid-wife, the old procedure could still lead to a programme whose form and content failed to represent precisely what the group wanted to show. This was a singular advance, but we could not afford to offer an all-film programme to more than one group in six, and even then it had to be shot on cheap film stock at a low shooting ratio, three to one. (By comparison, broadcasting professionals seldom work at less than 10 feet of film shot to one used.)

There was also an attempt to make 'selection' fairer. When I ran *Open Door* there was a waiting list of 600 groups (and individuals) for forty programmes a year. The Unit chose the groups during long afternoons of discussion that were a fearful burden on time and mind. The process made the election of a Pope look simple and was far too cumbersome to be described here. We knew it was as fair as we could make it, but it wasn't seen to be so. Public trust in the operation was important. I therefore set up a panel of 'observers'. This has been much modified since I left. But the difficulty of selecting for people's access to limited time will always remain in a broadcasting system.

Open Door was, and remains, very much in the margin of a television service, BBC-2, that in those days, even more than now, was itself a minority channel. And the programme budgets (under £1,000 for a thirty-minute programme when I took over) are always likely to be smaller than those of the mainstream output. Can the situation ever change so that every individual and group in the audience feels that in some way television represents their points of view?

The answer to that question must obviously be no, not on a

television system limited to three or four national channels. But even in this restricted situation things are improving. The Minorities Unit set up by London Weekend Television under Barry Cox has, with its *Skin* programme, given a voice to the black communities of Britain, even if it is largely London-based. It has also developed the professional skills of black broadcasters. The BBC continues not only with *Open Door* but also with its long-established Asian programme from Birmingham. Channel Four is committed to a better deal not only for the black communities but also for other small communities and women. But the limitations of broadcast television itself are about to be broken down.

What can the people of Britain expect by way of a broader representation of their interests, in video form, in what German television's Hans Kimmel has called the 'post-classical' television period of direct broadcast satellite, cable and video cassette? Though history never repeats itself, it may be said that we are poised at a moment similar to the time when, under Queen Anne in 1709, the Stationer's Company in this country lost its monopoly of book publishing. I would not like to stretch the analogy to imply that Tony Benn or the Glasgow Media Group are the equivalents of Milton in 1644, but there is no doubt that the voices raised against the monopoly of the broadcast institutions of this country, including 'authors' like independent producers and directors, have to a certain extent brought about the lifting of the limitations that is inherent in the setting up of Channel Four.

But, as with the rotary printing press, so with video cassette, cable and satellite; the new technological developments will interact with the ambitions of authors, entrepreneurs and the public will. The result will be a proliferation of voices, but the end of the mass audience, except for the basic services of news and some sport and entertainment programmes. The individual will have the responsibility of choosing his library by buying or renting cassettes or by purchasing access to particular cable channels.

The technical standards of broadcast television in the UK are very high. Our programmes are seen in all their detail and subtlety. But such standards require very costly equipment, and their cost is one of the factors that limit access to broadcast television. The great mass of people with something to say can't afford to make programmes in which to say it. We need paperback television to go with the hard-cover version. We can—and, on Channel Four, will—agree to lower standards in one or two known slots a week for the purpose of hearing the unheard voices, but that will only go some way towards solving the problem.

Cable TV could earmark whole channels, perhaps hundreds of hours a week, on which lower, cheaper technical standards were the accepted norm. Cable operations might be required in their franchise to make such channels—and even the equipment to construct the programmes—cheaply available on a first-come-first-served basis. And they would cost less for the subscribers to purchase.

In the word 'purchase' lies the great dilemma. Paul Fox pointed out on a *Did You See?* programme early in 1982 that even the BBC's extension of its rights to broadcast satellite programmes, paid for by subscription, created two classes of viewer: those who had the basic channels (presumably still paid for by licence or advertising), and those who could purchase viewing. I would go further and argue that access to specialized information and opinion will be as important for the individual at the start of the twenty-first century as ownership of property was at the start of the nineteenth. If we do not look very carefully at how we set up the new technologies, we are in grave danger of widening the national divide. There would be those who were able to receive a wide range of information and those with access to only a limited range. But how can we make commercial sense of the new technological opportunities while at the same time providing free and fair access to all available information? Will it take a latter-day Tony Benn to overrule television suppliers in a way that, while in charge of the Department of Energy, he overruled the Electricity and Gas Boards to allow people access to supplies even if they hadn't got the means to pay for them?

Perhaps the answer lies in an extension of the principles that we apply to education. Perhaps anybody with the will to ask should have free right of access to any video source. That would be a fearsome burden on the national economy. Maybe we should make all products available at local video libraries. But that would also cost a great deal, and would run counter to the energy-saving concept of bringing information to people's homes so that they do not have to travel to obtain it.

If a burden upon the state is unacceptable, can capitalism come to the rescue? What of the entrepreneurs? Will a new video Northcliffe seize opportunities that will leave Pearson Longman, Mitchell Beazley and Video Arts as far behind as Northcliffe left John

Walters's *Daily Universal Register*? If it were not for satellite, I would predict that in Britain we would come to the classic British compromise of the entrepreneur's market tempered by the needs of the people as interpreted by Government welfare statism. But satellite is international, and satellite is as much the wild card of information distribution as energy price is the wild card of international economics.

At this stage in the argument people usually interject that the internationalism of satellite development is limited by the language problem. But we are now very close the point at which where technology will be able to permit instant translation, either vocal or as subtitles. So we must settle for nothing less than a supranational organization that guarantees the free and fair availability of information to every member of a burgeoning world population. This is a wild vision, one that should be tempered by political reality. Many national Governments will fight rather than allow their subjects free access to information from other countries and other political systems. Nevertheless, thinking about the implications of satellite transmission of information perhaps requires us to aim for the stars.

UNESCO, which should be the forum where such things are discussed, has, ironically, most recently been the centre of attempts to *limit* the transmission of information from some countries to the rest of the world. Nevertheless, cheap access to the means to communicate and receive information must be our aim for everybody—anything less would be a betrayal of the opportunity that faces us. Fair and free distribution of all forms of information means positive regulation rather than deregulation. I for one would predict that the erstwhile terrestrial television broadcasters will combine to find a continuing role in the regulation of distribution—nationally and internationally—as well as of production for the information explosion. If they do not create a new role for themselves, they will die, and a deal of expertise will die with them. But if they survive, will they have the vision to promote controls so that they achieve fairness by supporting the voices that need to be heard and conveying their messages to those who want or need to hear rather than just to those who can afford to pay high prices to hear or be heard? Would Mr Singh, talking on a New Left Video Club tape or a low-cost cable service, ever reach an audience that included his hairdresser? Or will it all just be a Great New World of song contests and sport? We must all continue to work for the fairest possible access to, and distribution of, information within the limits of finance and political reality. And we must build into the new technology a form of regulation that encourages such fairness.

7. Cable Klondike

ROBERT MACNEIL

For one terrible week in the summer of 1976 I found myself a prisoner of television in New York, forced to stay in a hospital bed for a week, recovering from an operation. I had no desire to read and thus, supine and passive, I was the ideal television consumer. It was awful. Desperately I flipped my remote control up and down the seven available channels: six commercial, one public. Most of the time it was a choice between video drivel or sleep. I slept a lot.

Today I might be far more content to be that video captive. Assuming the hospital was connected to cable television, I could probably find a lot to stay awake for, certainly for one week. If they wish to pay for it, New Yorkers, at least those on Manhattan Island, can now have access to thirty television channels.

It is noon on Sunday, the doldrums of the TV schedule. I have just made a quick check of what is available on my service, Manhattan Cable TV.

Six feature films are running, ranging from old *Tarzan* and *Abbott and Costello* to a recent John Belushi comedy, *Continental Divide*. There are three church services, two sedate and traditional, the other an extravaganza from one of the new, so-called 'electronic' churches, linked nationally by satellite.

One channel is carrying live championship tennis, another a baseball game, another a profile of a rising black basketball star. The twenty-four hour news channel, Cable News Network, is relaying by satellite from Europe a live press conference by Secretary of State Alexander Haig. Two traditional networks, NBC and ABC, have news feature programmes. Two more channels are providing captioned news and sports scores, another constant weather reports. There is one programme in Japanese, another in Spanish. There is an academic discussion of Chinese philosophy and modern theories of

105

consciousness. I also encountered a programme called *Vision of Asia*; discussions of American Indian religious beliefs and antique oil lamps, an interview with Julie Andrews, a children's network showing an adventure serial made by Thames Television, a captioned classified advertisement channel with real estate and job offerings, and a community bulletin board announcing meetings and exhibitions.

A man who is tired of all that is probably not, as Dr Johnson said of London, tired of life, but he is probably very tired of television.

For this profusion I pay $23.25 (roughly £12) a month (calculated on an exchange rate of $2 to the pound). I could have it for $11.75 (£6), but I inherited the service from someone who also subscribed to Home Box Office, for which you pay an extra $11.50 a month. I could pay more: there is another subscription film channel called Cinemax, costing $12.50 (£6). And other pay channels, with arts and cultural offerings, are soon to be available. To put my present fee into perspective, $23.25 is now the price of one moderately good seat in a Broadway theatre or of a modest dinner for one in a New York restaurant, or of a largish book, say Henry Kissinger's memoirs.

The menu that I describe is just for noon on Sunday, one of the least attractive viewing periods of the week. By evening the cable will be embellished with sturdier fare, some exciting, some notorious. A gentleman called Ugly George regularly occupies one New York channel late at night with his own peculiar form of erotica. He wanders around Manhattan wearing a portable electronic camera and videotape recorder. He specializes in persuading women to undress for him, on camera, in alleys, doorways and the lobbies of buildings. He is particularly fascinated by breasts and behinds, which he records copiously. His programmes consist of the search, the encounter, the persuasion and, amazingly often, the surrender.

Another late-night feature on cable is softly pornographic. They do not quite do what Nancy Mitford's Hons called 'it', but almost. One night I witnessed what *Monty Python* might have conceived as a satire on the inane sports interview that is such a staple of American television. The participants were not vertical but horizontal—and naked. The only apparel worn by the male interviewer and his subject were neck microphones. Their topic: how different it was to act in German porno films as compared with American. They were very serious and, I thought, very boring. As they talked, delectable young ladies (who also happened to be lying around naked) occasionally caressed the participants, very distracting to me but not to these earnest seekers after truth. For protection, I tried to think of Robin Day.

Such extravagance is one consequence of the insouciant way in which America is crashing into the new broadcasting age, with cable to the fore. Cities award exclusive franchises to cable companies, usually demanding 5 per cent of their gross income as a fee. They impose conditions; they demand, for example, that some channels are reserved for public access, which means the opportunity for anyone to broadcast free of charge. So in Manhattan all those who felt disenfranchised or excluded by the traditional broadcasters can air what they like. What predominates is worthy, often impressive efforts by neighbourhood, religious, ethnic or interest groups: atheists and psychics, yogis and vegetarians, news from Harlem— and sex. That includes a programme offering a kind of dating service for homosexuals, as well as *Midnight Blue* and *The Ugly George Show*.

Another consequence is a Klondike atmosphere of frenzy and greed. Cable is America's fastest-growing industry. Fewer than one-third of American households have been connected to cable, and there is a rush to grab the rest. More are being wired at a rate of 250,000 a month. The industry is adding 2,000 new employees a month. Some 2,700 individual cable companies exist across the nation, some with a few thousand subscribers, the largest with hundreds of thousands.

To win the prized franchises for whole cities or parts of cities, cable companies have been promising the moon; cities have been demanding the earth. Very early cable services, dating from twenty years ago, were designed simply to improve picture reception from standard television broadcasters. A dozen channels were considered more than adequate. But improved technology has made it possible to offer dozens and dozens of channels. The Cox Cable Company recently contracted to provide the city of New Orleans with a basic subscriber service of 108 channels. It also promised a separate network linking hospitals and other city institutions, six local studios, one mobile production (outside broadcast) facility, thirty portable cameras, eighteen public access channels and a satellite uplink. Many cities are wary, however, because other cable companies have defaulted on more modest promises. Some important markets, like Chicago and Washington DC, have yet to seek franchise bids, and television viewers in those cities are simply doing without cable in the meantime.

Cable companies are fighting back, claiming that the demands that cities are making will bankrupt them. Through their national association, cable companies are trying to get Congress to pass a national Bill to ease their financial burden. But Washington is not in a mood to meddle in the new communications revolution. For years the expansion of cable television was held back by Federal regulations. In 1979 the Federal Communication Commission (FCC) lifted those regulations and with President Reagan in the White House the atmosphere is even less restrictive. The new religion is deregulation, a *laissez-faire* attitude toward the emerging communications technologies.

President Carter's FCC chairman, Charles Ferris, who began this trend, called his policy 'Darwinian'. The Government, he declared, would open the gates to all forms of new communications technology and would let them compete in the marketplace. The public was better able to choose what should survive, Ferris reasoned, than Government regulators. So Washington is now letting the marketplace choose what should prosper among cable, conventional broadcasters, subscription television, direct satellite to home transmission and home video recording systems.

According to Les Brown, the editor of *Channels* magazine, 'While other advanced countries, with all the same technology available to them, are proceeding cautiously (most have not yet authorized cable, domestic satellites, or any form of pay television, and still have far fewer over-the-air channels than we), the US is going wild with media.' Brown, who is one of the most thoughtful observers of the media scene in America, is worried by the assumption that consumers will choose what is in the public interest. 'Market forces, being nothing new, have a bad track record,' he says. 'There can be no expectation that unregulated television will provide much more than pap, albeit in greater quantities than before.'

So far the evidence on the home screen belies him, but everyone agrees that these are very early days. It is widely expected that there will be many casualties along the way before the dust settles and we can see which are the fittest that have survived.

For all the billions of dollars the cable companies are confidently investing in wiring up the nation—$14,000 (£7,000) a mile in the tidy suburbs, $100,000 (£50,000) a mile in the big cities—a lot of doubts have begun to surface. Some are asking whether cable will prove to be the technology that survives, or whether it will be bypassed before half the nation is wired. This is the decade of cable, the industry trumpets, meaning that profitable Nirvana has arrived. Others say that cable will last only this decade: it will be obsolete before it is complete.

Four principal competitors are beginning to give cable company executives the shivers at four in the morning.

One is the tendency of big apartment complexes and housing developments to create do-it-yourself cable systems. The skies over America are already filled with television beamed up, down and across the nation by an elaborate system of domestic satellites. By mid-1982 there were no fewer than forty-seven different programme services available by satellite to cable companies. A dozen more were planned for the end of the year. For $10,000 (£5,000) an apartment complex can install its own receiver dish and provide all its residents with TV service. It is vastly cheaper for one apartment owner to buy a programming service and then decide whether to charge the tenants or give them the service like a utility. Either way, the loser is the local cable company that has paid heavily for the franchise in that area. The development also has public policy implications; the hiving-off of middle-class apartment dwellers may make it uneconomic for cable operators to provide service to poorer areas. The city of Dallas, Texas, illustrates the point. There 82 per cent of the new housing construction permits that are issued are for multiple dwelling units (that is, blocks of flats). The significance of the threat is clear.

Another threat to cable companies comes from broadcasters offering subscriber television. Broadcasters can now scramble the signals they transmit. They can be decoded (the industry word is 'descrambled') by a small box attached to the subscriber's television set. In cities where there is no cable television, thousands of Americans are now paying $30 (£15) a month or so for quality films or exclusive sports events. Some entrepreneurs are even buying or leasing small TV stations for this purpose. The developing technology holds the promise of splitting one TV signal to provide two or more channels.

A refinement of this challenge to cable TV is being tried experimentally in New York. A prominent local television station will transmit, during the night, several hours of exceptional programming. Paying subscribers will receive it on home video taperecorders, timed to operate while they sleep but governed by a descrambler. That descrambler may be one installed by a technician or a disposable one that arrives by mail, dies after operating for a week and must be renewed. Cable companies may lose subscribers who prefer this arrangement, since their own videotape package can be replayed in 'prime times' of their choosing.

Cable operators have already noted, although they do not advertise the fact, that their rate of penetration into Americans homes is still modest. In areas where cable has been installed 45 per cent of American homes on average refuse to subscribe. Even worse, in areas where over-the-air reception is good, cable penetration drops to 25 per cent. Some cable companies, competing now for valued franchises and for exciting programme services, are projecting penetration rates as high as 70 per cent. According to *Emmy*, a magazine published by the National Academy of Television Arts and Science. 'They're dreaming.' Anything that lures potential subscribers away weakens their penetration. Some cable companies are already worried that it may take seven or eight years' worth of monthly subscriptions to recoup the millions they have spent on wiring a community. Some are worried that there may be no 'pay-back', or profit, at the end of the line, especially if they have to pay very high interest rates on their venture capital.

Barron's, the influential financial weekly published by Dow Jones, says cable is a 'billion-dollar gamble' because it faces 'more competition than any medium in any market has ever had to face'. The newspaper adds: 'The breadth and intensity of the rivalry for both viewers and ad dollars—to say nothing of the splintered, specialized markets rapidly emerging—makes long-range projections of profitability very iffy.'

A third potent threat that many see is Direct Broadcasting by Satellite (DBS). The technology exists here as in the United Kingdom, and as soon as a new generation of satellites with higher transponding power can be launched, millions of American roofs are expected to start sprouting small receiver dishes. Home subscribers will then pay for the appropriate descrambling boxes on their television sets and, theoretically, they will have direct access to unlimited products. Picture quality is expected to be better than that provided by cable transmission. DBS will probably not be feasible until 1984, but it is close enough to make some cities now pondering cable franchise decisions wonder whether they should wait for the next half-generation of technology to arrive.

Finally, there is another threat to cable, the phone company. AT&T, the American Telephone and Telegraph Company, is the world's largest corporation. For years it has enjoyed a virtual monopoly over basic telephone services in the USA and Canada. In exchange for that monopoly, it has agreed not to use its enormous wealth to compete in data-processing, computer technologies and other fields of telecommunications. Now all that is changing. 'Ma Bell', as the giant is known, has been offered a new arrangement: it will be broken up, by divesting itself of its twenty-two regional phone companies (mini-giants in themselves), and in return will be allowed to get into other fields like computers and videocommunications.

Now, ATT just happens to have a wire into virtually every home in the United States as it is. The phone wires do not have the technical capacity to carry a colour TV picture, but they could easily carry much of the other information cable is promising, designed to make each home a place where one can shop, bank and seek information.

Cable operators in Coral Gables, Florida, are experimenting with these services, but the application is limited because it requires two-way facilities. Customers must be able to send signals back, and the majority of cable systems are one-way. But the AT&T lines are already two-way—obviously, since that is how people dial out—and their capacity could easily be improved. The worried president of the National Cable Television Association, Tom Wheeler, using the industry's jargon, puts it this way: 'AT&T can do the same things with long lines today in broadband that they did with long lines in twisted pairs unless someone says, "Wait stop!"' Only the cable industry is saying that, and the chairman of AT&T, Charles Brown, is saying that the new 'Ma Bell' intends to compete vigorously in some of these areas. (The most likely area is the provision of printed, not picture, information in the home.) Wheeler says it is vital for cable to know what AT&T is planning because its actions 'will determine whether or not we (the cable industry) get to tomorrow'.

As if all these risks weren't enough, the cable gold-rushers have another headache. Paradoxically, they are short of channel space. Most of the cable systems already in operation are out of date. Of all present cable systems, 62 per cent, in more than half of all cabled homes, have twelve channels or fewer. Since they are required to carry available television signals in the area and provide public

111

access, that leaves only a few extra channels for attractive or lucrative pay programmes. As franchises across the country expire and come up for renewal, a number of cities are making it a condition of renewal that the cable company install state-of-the-art technology. That is the equivalent of installing an entire new system at great expense. Few cable companies are rushing to upgrade their systems voluntarily. Yet restricted channels make it difficult to both attract new subscribers and advertising to the channels that they have.

Advertising revenue is still low. In 1981 cable television had advertising revenues of only $129 million dollars; network advertising revenues were $5.3 billion. While cable ad revenues are expected to increase as more homes are linked up, it is not expected that they will pose a significant threat to conventional broadcasters. Cable ad revenues may be as high as $3.1 billion in 1991, while broadcast network ad revenues are projected to reach $16.4 billion.

Advertisers' reluctance to plunge more enthusiastically into cable underlines two further apparent weaknesses of the new system as organized in the United States. The multiplicity of cable companies means that few systems reach very large numbers of homes. To do so, they must link up with other systems to form cable networks or subscribe to national programming services. Although that is happening to some extent, the numbers reached are still low by conventional broadcast standards.

Then there is the relative invisibility of cable programming. At present it can be difficult to find out what is being carried on cable. Some cable operators provide programme guides, but the newspapers can't be bothered and other commercial publications list only highlights. Particularly for the public-access channels, the only reliable way to find out what's happening is to switch around the dial. In addition, there is very little paid advertising or promotion. So in its present stage of development American cable may offer a programmer a far better chance of getting his programme broadcast than does conventional TV but a considerably smaller chance of getting it seen or heard.

That, in turn, affects what cable can spend on creating programmes. So far, even the biggest cable companies have been able to spend far less on creating original programming than their network counterparts. According to *Channels* magazine, a typical network variety show lasting an hour costs $850,000. Cable is willing to spend an average of $250,000 for an equivalent show.

112

Clearly, although the United States has rushed into cable ahead of Britain and every other country, it is too early to say what impact the development will have on television viewing and what that will mean to society when it settles down. It may be ten years, assuming benign neglect persists in Washington, before the Darwinian fittest have survived the rigours of the marketplace.

Informed Americans have been trying to penetrate the welter of jargon and hype to isolate some implications for the public interest. First, the quality of programming: will the unregulated proliferation of channels serve the people well?

There are two schools of thought about how much diversity will survive, or to what extent cable will be forced by market pressures to resemble the traditional fare on American network television. To the extent that choice has been restricted by the scarcity of channels, unfettered cable is a clear step towards more choice. But to the extent that viewer choice has been restricted merely by the exigencies of commercial competition (audience maximizing), it is not clear that multi-channel cable will significantly improve the choice, if all is left to the marketplace. In mass communications the market forces may restrict choice. Cable will certainly offer simulated choice, choice in the superficials. Perhaps that will be important in consumer sovereign democracies.

ABC Inc., owner of one of the three TV networks and the most profitable, said in its most recent annual report that, 'In the future only those who can profit from a small audience will be able to profit at all.' Since ABC has profited enormously, until now, from doing precisely the opposite, from maximizing its audience to the hilt, the prophecy has a certain piquancy. It is gospel for those who believe in 'narrowcasting' as opposed to broadcasting—the shaping of programmes to appeal to a selected slice of the mass audience (what parts of the BBC have been doing for years, as has public broadcasting in the USA). Success for 'narrowcasting' is the fervent wish of those who believe much American television has been corrupted by its slavish pursuit of mass audience, which has required all programming to be the product of lowest-common-denominator taste.

People in the industry who think this is how things will 'shake out' expect that of some sixty national programme services available to cable this year, the ones that attempt to duplicate the broad appeal of over-the-air TV, are doomed. They believe that the narrowly focused services, like the all-news network, children's programming or special cultural services, will survive. They like to draw an analogy from what happened to the American magazine industry. A generation ago there were a number of magazines with national circulations in the millions, like the *Saturday Evening Post, Life* and *Colliers.* Television wiped them out. Now the magazine industry thrives anew through diversification, and hundreds of magazines find it profitable to publish for discreet segments of the market. If the *New Yorker* can maintain its enviable editorial standards in fiction and journalism on a circulation of 505,000 and wax fat with the glossiest advertising, why can't its equivalent in television? Certainly I am one who would wish it that way.

Consider the opposite possibility, however. In earlier years people subscribed to cable for one reason only: they wanted to get the ghosts off their TV screens, and cable offered better reception. Now it is different. Tom Wheeler, head of the Cable Television Association says, 'Eighty-five per cent of cable subscribers just subscribe in order to get movies without commercials.' According to *Channels* magazine: 'Seven million Americans spent close to $2 billion in 1981 for pay television, mostly to watch movies they used to see at their neighborhood theatres.'

Another indicator of American mass taste is the fact that in 1982 Americans were spending three times as much on the new electronic games that can be played through small computers on home television sets as they were spending on films at the box office. To exploit this craze some cable channels are offering such games to subscribers at prices that are lower than the purchase price of the cassettes.

But the more specialized services that cable now offers are not sufficient bait to justify extra charges. It is an open question, and may be so for some years, how much serious cultural traffic the new system will bear. The most ambitious so far, CBS Cable, offers an intelligent but safe mix of middle-brow classical music, plays, dance and talk. It lost $20 million in 1981 and is expected to repeat that in 1982. Two other cultural channels, ABC/Hearst's Arts and one called Bravo, are both also losing money.

The newest service in this area, the Entertainment Channel, which has close links with British television, is going out of its way to deny that it is a cultural channel lest it frighten subscribers away. The

Entertainment Channel made big news, when it was first announced, by signing a ten-year-contract with the BBC for exclusive first use of BBC programmes. Until now such programmes, from the old *Forsyte Saga* to the complete plays of Shakespeare, have been a mainstay of public television. It was widely assumed that the blow to public broadcasting might be fatal. But the forces of the marketplace have proved that much BBC material may be too highbrow for the Entertainment Channel, which planned to emphasize more of the BBC's mass-audience material. The *New York Times* observed that much of the planned material would be similar to that available on network television and wondered how many people would want to pay the extra $8–$12 a month for this one service.

In short, whether this proliferation of cultural programming can pay for itself, when divided among so many commercial cable channels and public television, remains to be seen. If the answer is yes, in a few years' time the American experiment will have been gloriously vindicated on that score. If the forces of the marketplace demand more mass-appeal programming to meet the high initial costs of cable, it will have failed. Such failure might demonstrate that the arts are better subsidized and better disseminated by a greater concentration of resources, whether public or commercial.

As for news, cable has already inspired a minor revolution. Ted Turner's Cable News Network has panicked the three big networks, ABC, CBS, and NBC, into an extraordinary expansion of their news services, most notably some form of all-night news service, for fear that their affiliate stations might be seduced by the material Turner offers. But this is a preliminary skirmish.

The real crunch in news will come if cable is such a success that it cuts into network income and makes it uneconomic to maintain the huge, worldwide news services of CBS, NBC and ABC. They are the main arbiters of journalistic quality and integrity on American television. Without them, TV journalism could rapidly degenerate as local commercial television has in a number of places, where competition has often turned news into silly entertainment. But even optimistic projections of cable income do not suggest that. The networks and their news departments look secure for a long time.

The final area to consider is access. Here there is no doubt that the advent of cable has, so far, brought some improvement.

The interests of older Americans, women, religious denominations, clubs, as well as racial, ethnic and linguistic

115

minorities, can be explicitly and purposefully served. What does that achieve, beyond gratifying the egos of those who make the broadcasts? No matter. To consider the question fairly, cable forces professional broadcasters, like me, to adopt a different viewpoint, to abandon our elitist attitudes and see access television as the service it is. These programmes are necessarily so amateurishly produced, so anonymously broadcast and viewed presumably by so few people that their impact will be very different from that of the broadcasting we are used to. In New York City the Chinese, Japanese, Spanish, Russian, German, and Serbian-Croatian speakers must be delighted with the channels that serve them. Clearly, all these are beneficiaries, as are the high-school football and baseball teams whose exploits are lovingly covered by community-access television.

There are those who believe that such extreme 'narrowcasting' will help to foster the sense of community that has been diluted by other forces in society, including the fear of crime. But early experiments with access, pioneered in New York City, have demonstrated a truth that I failed to see at one time: television is a communications medium in the widest sense. You need not be an expert or a professional to use it, provided there are many channels.

There is another kind of public access that benefits from cable, and that is access for the US House of Representatives, soon perhaps the Senate, and scores of state legislatures, city councils and county boards of supervisors. Until the arrival of cable, such bodies received television attention only at moments of notoriety. The decision of Morton Grove, a small town in Illinois to ban all guns, for example, brought the national media down on it. With cable, if Morton Grove wished, its Town Council or Board of Education could be routinely covered.

As for the national legislature, I have run into a surprising number of Americans across the country who subscribe to, and pay to watch, the live coverage of the House of Representatives on a channel called C-Span. Without cable such coverage would survive only as brief excerpts in news bulletins. With multiple-channel cable the worthy representatives can talk away all day, astonishing the heavens on the way up to the satellite and down again, and are heard in thousands of homes.

As usual in the United States, advancing technology far outstrips our understanding of its implications. Like the motor car, it is slammed into service as soon as it works, and if, in the process, it transforms society, historians and social scientists can pick up the pieces in years to come. This is not a society to mull things over very carefully first. Technology knocks insistently at the door, distracting the thinkers.

There may be great social risk in this new leap because it puts such a premium on the ability to pay for service. Until now most American television could at least masquerade as free; the cost of the $6 billion a year in advertising support wore a million tiny disguises in the prices of soap powder and frozen peas. Now diversity beckons those who can pay not only to be better entertained but also perhaps to be better informed.

The prestigious Aspen Institute has thought about this issue in a preliminary way and worries that this new era 'may create increasing social stratification, structural unemployment and other obstacles to a fair and stable society'. The Aspen people look ahead to a time when such systems might be used, for example, to deliver mail electronically. And they ask a question that may have far wider applications: 'Will the new, serving the few, accelerate the decline of the old, which were meant to serve the many?'

It is a good question, but the policy-makers in Washington are not asking it.

8. *Cards on the Table*

STEPHEN HEARST

Although Britain launched the first public television service in the world in 1936, television itself did not achieve intellectual respectability or recognition until the late 1960s. Until then television was watched by the servants; when there were no more servants, by the nannies; when those disappeared, by the children, under strictly controlled conditions. If the intelligentsia's family income did not rise to servants or nannies, what mattered was the location of the television set. It was never in the sitting-room; it was either 'upstairs' or 'downstairs'. When in 1954 I attempted to script a BBC television documentary about Oxford, I was treated (although I was endowed with voting rights to elect, for example, a Professor of Poetry) like a minor but indisputably bad smell. Special permission was graciously given to film the college tortoise at Oriel. New College withheld permission for the participation of its choir.

Mankind's progress, it was argued, from the cave drawings of Altamira and Lascaux, via Kant, to the analysis of language as a precondition of philosophical rigour, had been long and tortuous. It was the possession and subsequent refinement of language that distinguished us from the beasts. Would not the ascendancy of visual sequences on television take us back to the caves? By the end of the 1960s, however, some of the best drama to be seen and heard in Britain had been written not for the theatre but for the television screen. Television situation comedy united our exceedingly class-conscious nation in almost universal laughter. Men of great distinction increasingly lent their authority and time to political, cultural and scientific programmes. The British broadcasting system managed to grow, largely from its own seeds, that very rare plant, sustained quality programming. Rubbish, too, there was in plenty, as there is today. To fill the unforgiving minute with sixty seconds' worth of memorabilia would require the constant presence and application of genius. What is available is talent, so that a day rarely passes in Britain during which no programme is transmitted that is, at the very least, good of its kind.

How this talent came to gather in Britain and not in France, or Germany or Italy (where public-service criteria have also prevailed in national broadcasting policies) is itself a fascinating story. There was, first of all, the prestige the BBC had acquired, both at home and abroad, during the Second World War. The launching of the Third Programme in 1946 provided additional proof that the BBC took seriously its triple duties to inform, educate and entertain. Some of the brightest sparks from the four corners of the Commonwealth did not then take a very sanguine view of the creative capacities latent in their respective homelands and found the inevitable friction between their own cultural assumptions and those of the mother country rather fruitful. The Empire had survived the war, just, and was, over the next two decades, to give up the ghost as gracefully as it could. Many young men and women who might in other times have wanted to serve it looked for alternatives that to them held fascination and interest. In addition, that extraordinary phenomenon, the unspoken but powerful prejudice against business and industry, was prevalent in British university life. It would be a caricature of a complex careers comparison to say that whereas a promising German graduate would seek a career in German industry, his British counterpart would try for the Civil Service or the BBC; nevertheless, it is a caricature with more than a grain of truth in it. The quality of applicants to the BBC then being exceedingly high, it needs to be said that selection procedures were shrewd and fair. The Television Service itself was small; its hours of transmission were negligible by comparison with those of three national radio networks; and what turned out to constitute its pioneering staff was concentrated in just one or two buildings, where it became, in essence, a pressure-cooker for new television conventions, programme ideas and formats.

One cannot exaggerate the importance of team-work in quality television—and not just team-work but also the need for each member of the team to have considerable talent for his or her specific task. Technologically speaking, television is a difficult, complex and demanding medium, requiring a vast diversity of skills. The form is hard to handle, and unless you are very careful, it can easily dominate the content of programmes. (In this respect, it differs greatly from

119

radio, where form and content are in more easily manageable balance.) For example, it is symptomatic of the difficulty that content permanently faces in asserting itself on television that playwrights complain of the vast teams that are assembled to produce the creative result of a single mind and sensibility, of a single pen and relatively few sheets of paper. They rarely complain of the use that radio makes of their work. There the apparatus is small, and the imagination of the listener often supplies what dozens of designers, lighting engineers, cameramen, make-up artists—to mention 'team positions' at random—strive to achieve. Shelley's poetry needed Shelley alone, the writing of *The Pickwick Papers* none other than Dickens. To put a single close-up of a face on television has, up till now, needed dozens of people. Even greatly simplified technology is not very likely to reduce television staff input by a significant amount. Yes, the trick *can* be done by fewer people, as it is in many countries, but I doubt if it can be done well.

Television, if it aspires to be taken seriously by serious people, if it seeks the excellence that doctors, lawyers and engineers take for granted in their professional aspirations, needs a creative mass of talent to serve it. This creative mass need not be concentrated in a capital city, but it is most likely to be found and kept there. Small countries with small populations are thus placed at a great disadvantage, by comparison with large ones, in seeking to achieve a home-grown television output of quality. The gods hovering over television are, like the word itself, of mixed Greek and Roman origin; they have not heard of the doctrine of fairness. I do not know of a single small country that can claim a sustained daily output of quality television programmes, let alone of quality programmes produced by itself alone. That is not to look at the television world in what trendies would call 'imperialist' or 'racist' terms. Unfortunately, it is necessary to make that clear, since the possession of television, like that of national airlines, has become a status symbol for nationhood. There are many large nations that have so far produced little in the way of quality television broadcasting and many small ones that surface with the occasional gem that bags an Italia Prize. The emphasis of this argument lies in sustained capacity to maintain high programme standards. Nor will I here engage in any dialogue that counters this point with the cultural relativism, 'Who is to decide what is good or bad on television and who are you to tell us?' Just spend a couple of days in a United States hotel outside Manhattan

Island and a few more of the big cities, turn on your television set and then compare what you have seen with what is on offer in the United Kingdom.

What we have achieved in television in this country we ought not to take for granted. We aim constantly at excellence and occasionally achieve it, irrespective of whether we are funded by public money through the licence fee or through advertising, despite the competitive stance that both sides have adopted. There are few instances in which wooing a popular audience for its custom has not resulted in the lowering of standards. And it is not difficult to envisage how the programme standards we have achieved since 1936 could be lowered in a mere fraction of that time. Technological means of transmission are no longer scarce. The critical mass of talent that has hitherto served three British television channels could disperse if there were many more and if video discs and video cassettes of dubious quality but guaranteed profit-making capacity arrived in quantity on the open market. Regulation has shielded British television from Sir Thomas Gresham and his law. The siren voices of deregulation will warble agreeably and ably, you may be sure; if ever they achieve their objective, it will be too late to complain.

Exacting programme standards derive from clearly thought-out broadcasting policies, carried out by highly talented programme-makers who pool their various talents at different moments in the course of production. Unfortunately, the viewing public has never displayed the faintest interest in policies and judges programmes in isolation from the policies from which they derive or, worse, in terms of the personalities who appear on our screens. Thus, none of the television developments in the United Kingdom owes anything to expressions of public opinion. The advent of commercial television was the consequence of the Conservative Party's dislike of monopoly and the influence of a powerful lobby within that party. BBC-2 made its appearance earlier than the BBC wished because of governmental pressures. Channel Four cannot remotely claim to owe its existence to public demand, and the coming of satellite broadcasting in 1986 can be traced to combined political and broadcasting anxiety not to be outsmarted by foreign interests in space. Thus, broadcasting policy in the United Kingdom is, and always has been, in the hands of very few people indeed, although its consequences touch every household in the country. It is easy to impugn the motives of the broadcasters who are now in charge, to accuse them of declaring, 'What we have we hold.' In reality, like other fallible mortals, they act from mixed motives. They are richly experienced in the strengths and weaknesses of their colleagues abroad and generally conclude from their experience that Britain has done remarkably well in this field and is acknowledged to have done well by those friends abroad who know the score. They would like to see the present programme standards upheld and the new technology used to enrich existing choices rather than to upset and destroy all present arrangements.

Let me give just one example of the virtues of present arrangements that we all take for granted and that could easily disappear in the fervour for pluralism that some of the British media front-runners espouse. We take it as natural that all public-service broadcasting should offer the same or equivalent fare to all our viewers, wherever they happen to live. It would not occur to us to restrict the televising of the wedding of the Prince of Wales or of the Wimbledon Lawn Tennis Championships or of the FA Cup Final to one part of the kingdom while denying it to others. Yet in the case of outstanding sporting events it is fairly predictable that precisely such a thing might come about. Virtually all sporting bodies are short of money, and many top events might have dropped out of the sporting calendar if they had not been rescued by tobacco or insurance companies. These sporting bodies will find it hard to resist the offer of future cable companies to buy exclusivity of coverage in exchange for sums that are beyond the capacities of ITV or the BBC to pay. Exclusivity could be used by cable interests as their single most potent attraction to their potential subscribers. We would then have created different classes of viewer. Contrast this possibility with the categorical pledge given by the BBC that it would use its two satellite broadcasting channels, from 1986 onwards, entirely for the enrichment, and not the diminution, of choice. There is a good deal to worry about here, and we must surely keep our political wits about us to prevent the best features of today's broadcasting from becoming a nostalgic memory tomorrow. Distrust, in particular, the cries for freedom and always ask, 'Freedom for whom?' It could be that my freedom to extend my fist should rightly end *before*, and not *after*, it touches the tip of your nose.

I have deliberately used the term 'mass' in the opposite sense to that in which it is used in the context of the medium of television itself. Little else has done television as much harm as to be called a 'mass medium'. The same programme may indeed be seen by half the population of the country at the same time, but viewing *conditions* do not merge these millions into a mass. In a real mass individual components must not only share an experience; they must also be in physical contact with one another. A football crowd constitutes a mass—its gestures, raucous chants, corporate swaying represent behaviour that very few of its individual human atoms would ever exhibit on their own. Whereas a packed cinema audience can represent a mass, television reaches a couple of people in their own home. The response of millions of viewers, watching the same programme in their homes, is never the response of a mass. The mass orator, Aneurin Bevan, for example, who could hold a crowd or the House of Commons spellbound, never achieved the same effect over the fragmented audiences that saw the same image because the essential physical contact was missing and because only that contact can condone rhetoric. On television a whisper can produce a greater effect. 'Mass', to my way of thinking, suggests a collectivity that individuals, added together for the purposes of television audience measurement, never display. All you can say is that a given number of people watched a certain programme; the larger the audience, the less likely it is that their collective appreciation will have been very high. That is why audience measurement by itself is a fairly meaningless exercise, on which, for all sorts of fatuous reasons, much competitive meaning has been bestowed, particularly by journalists writing for the popular press. Yet this very exercise has been boosted by an interpretation of 'mass' that is, as applied to television, fallacious.

Paradoxically, the communications gurus have generally looked only at the final product and seldom at the production end. Had they searched properly there, they would at last have encountered their mass, namely all the boys and girls who nowadays tend to shorten their Christian names and enjoy a very short-lived glory on the long—and ever longer—television credit rollers. For all those Mikes and Sues and Bobs to give of their best, they need broadcasting policies that bestow on them a generous amount of trust and hence freedom, clear leadership, adequate money—and a suitable broadcasting architecture. This last requirement has, to my uncertain knowledge, never been discussed at all in broadcasting analyses. It is not enough to gather a creative mass of television talent together; you have also got to house it so that the sparks do not die down but eventually burst into a strictly controlled flame. Broadcasting House in Portland Place not only shuts people off from one another, but it also expresses, in its secretive divisions of thick and irregular walls, some of radio's salient characteristics. Whenever there is talk of accommodation changes in Broadcasting House, Drama and Talks producers will summon up deep emotion to prove to you that their work would be shipwrecked beyond hope of recovery if they were made to share an office with their secretaries. In television it would be odd for producers to prefer such solitary intellectual confinement.

Hence there is a great deal in the shape of television's working places that influences the quality of the programmes that are conceived therein. Not only should dozens of practitioners in one particular discipline be housed together, but also the building should be large enough to accommodate at least two other disciplines, so that shared technical facilities, clubs and canteens lead to constant meetings. In such circumstances cross-fertilization is much more likely than cross-sterilization. (By contrast, the best places to meet people in Broadcasting House are the lifts connecting the eight floors; there I once introduced two people who had worked in the building for twenty-five years without ever meeting one another.) But if, in the interests of regional devolution, only one or two producers from a particular television discipline are placed in a regional headquarters, it requires quite outstanding self-generating impulses of creativity on their part to match, not to say exceed, the programme standards of their colleagues back in the metropolis who hunt in packs. It is not devolution itself that is in question, but the numbers of staff used to make it effective. That is why frank programme discussion of regional (or national regional) programmes is always inhibited: the metropolitan reviewer (who frequently happens also to be a network controller) deducts his own guilt at having made too little money available from his low expectations of a first-class result. The final arithmetic of this equation often amounts to silence. The bigger battalions do, on the whole, consistently produce the best work in television, yet big battalions will remain rare. Every new technological development points towards smaller units. Impasse.

We may see a gradual deterioration in television programme standards as outlets multiply, but that is not inevitable. Another way to tackle the problem is to look at the vital stages of programme-making. In drama and light entertainment the final outcome is predictable early on; it depends on the quality both of the script and of the editorial judgement brought to bear on that script. Production can save or enhance the script; it cannot do without it or replace it. In most other television disciplines the final shape and content of a given programme are much less predictable. Some portions of programmes take weeks, others merely minutes, to assemble. It is often difficult to judge whether the narrative thrust, which in a linear medium provides the necessary continuity, has been maintained until a fairly advanced stage of the production. By that time, the producer is in danger of being over-familiar with his material. A fresh editorial eye is often vital to the eventual success or failure of the whole operation, and such an eye is provided by a good executive producer. The rise of the independent producer (or would it be more accurate to speak of the conversion of the dependent producer?) and the probable mushrooming of small production units could well lead to the fatal neglect of the role of the executive producer, whose contribution to the success of British television is one of the better kept professional secrets of the last two decades.

The technological multiplication of means, with its immense need for additional software, is likely to make many a talented television programme-maker feel that his hour has struck, that his crock of gold is there for the collecting. The Fates that guard all electronic endeavours are, despite the rise of a more merciful religion, much the same as those that dealt with Prometheus, and I rather think they murmur, 'Beware.' Not only does television at its best need the pooling of talents and resources, but its relative scarcity until now has meant that sizeable national audiences would watch what at first sight might appear esoteric or unpopular programmes. Whereas the poet or the novelist has to strive for recognition through many works and often over many years, existing television distribution can ensure fame for the practitioner overnight. It is very tempting to ascribe such fame to one's talent alone, and to ignore the effects of the technology. Multiply the channels, fragment the audiences and you are bound to reduce the spell that performers and practitioners alike have managed to cast over their public. More important, however, the assumption that more television will mean more of those programmes that we are at present particularly proud of needs to be looked at good and hard.

The American example of broadcasting by cable is constantly cited but has comparatively little relevance to the United Kingdom broadcasting scene. Broadcasting in the United States is first and last a business, its prime purpose being the making of money. If you regard the programmes as interruptions in a stream of commercials— we take the opposite view—you have got to hand it to the Americans: they are fulfilling their primary aim quite brilliantly. The success of cable diffusion in the United States is partly a protest against picture quality that is inferior in most respects to the one that we enjoy, as a matter of course, in Western Europe; it is also partly a reaction against the inescapable sales drive of the television networks and the arid sameness of much of the programming. This will not be the case in Britain. There are two, possibly three, strands of cable programmes that are likely to have enough audience appeal in this country to persuade people either to pay monthly subscriptions to enjoy additional television channels or to pay for individual programmes on an ad hoc basis. These are feature films, sports coverage and pornographic material. Since broadcasting policies are always discussed by potential franchise candidates with a high-mindedness that makes you think of Mammon using make-up to look like St Francis, it might be as well to separate the humbug from the real substance in the new technology arguments.

Why protect broadcasting by regulation at all now that the scarcity of technological means is about to vanish? We do not regulate publishing, so what is so special about broadcasting? Is not the exercise of freedom infinitely more important than the protection of existing broadcasting standards? Is it not time to abolish the nanny state?

Broadcasting, unlike publishing, is expensive and will remain expensive. To invest, at the very minimum, £1,500 million would entitle prospective investors to dream of, shall we say, sizeable returns. To realize these, they would need to offer a sceptical public something that it does not enjoy at present or to take away something it does enjoy in order to reserve it for subscribers on an exclusive basis. To take the FA Cup Final or the Grand National away from the general public, to whom these national events are almost birthrights, in order to give it to subscribers in some of Britain's larger cities would not be the easiest or most persuasive of public relations exercises to carry out. Far better, then, to talk of freedom without specifying its potential spread. Those who conjure up glittering operatic galas or relays from theatres, to be financed by minorities on a pay-as-you-view basis, must first demonstrate how profits would be created by programmes made for majority tastes, for it is those tastes that underpin every financial speculation in broadcasting. The analogy with book publishing is profoundly misleading, because book publishing itself is largely a cultural minority pursuit; low investment and restricted circulation for a given title are still sustainable.

Regulation, on closer inspection, turns out to be more than the last-ditch defence for existing institutional interests. Your freedom may impinge on mine. Moreover, one of the secrets of good television programming is the continuing discovery of new broadcasting veins. As with the mining of minerals, you need to sink a number of exploratory shafts before you discover the gold in them there hills. If there is anything one can say with a fair degree of certainty about any largely or purely commercial broadcasting venture, it is that it must seek to identify the prevalent majority viewing taste and, by serving that taste, to reinforce it. When an American station owner tells you that he is acting more democratically than you, the elitist Limey programme-maker, because he has found out what the public wants and is providing it round the clock, your answer must be that his public can only want what it already gets until it sees something different and decides whether it wants that or not. Fifteen years ago in Britain you might have been thought potty if you had predicted the current national craze for snooker.

What, then, would constitute my own ideal hand for the future of British broadcasting? One by one, here are my cards on the table.

First, the existing broadcasting organizations will have to justify their continued existence by the excellence of the service they render to the nation through the quality, variety and balance of their programmes. If they are deemed to discharge their duties well, both in the eyes of the public and in the opinion of its elected representatives, then the means to enable them to carry on must be provided through the retention of the licence fee for the BBC and advertising for the commercial sector.

Second, the political and cultural wits of the nation should be engaged in defeating the operation of Sir Thomas Gresham's law, which states that bad currency will always drive out the good. The best way to do this is to adopt the term 'enrichment' as a national broadcasting objective in making use of the new technology in the late 1980s and early 1990s. This means that we do not allow cable and satellite broadcasting to grow at the expense of the existing arrangements but instead encourage these new means of information distribution to provide us with extra choice. How, precisely?

Third, broadcasting freedom needs to be defended, nourished and redefined. Freedom for the highest bidder to operate a broadcasting franchise would mean that the public air was no longer a precious commodity but an article for sale. Regulation is essential. It must both prohibit *and* allow. For every 'Thou shalt not' there must be a corresponding 'Thou shalt'. The fact that we have an audience of millions for a programme on antiques, for example, is due to existing broadcasting obligations; it would be virtually unthinkable if we laboured under a commercial free-for-all on the American pattern. Whether regulatory functions are carried out by the old guardians of the existing dispensation or by some new ones for cable and satellite broadcasting is but a secondary consideration, the primary being the recognition that publishing freedom and broadcasting freedom are essentially different in kind. Because of the costs involved and the attendant risks, broadcasting freedom at all times needs a little help.

Fourth, broadcasting policy is too important to be left to politicans and broadcasters to brood over in private. The issues are not all that complicated, and a fresh draught of public opinion could do no harm in an area into which it has hardly ever penetrated. At present, people at large exercise their critical faculties on programmes but approach broadcasting policy with a mixture of innocence and ignorance. Policy should more often become the subject of programmes on both radio and television.

Fifth, the uses of cable need to be integrated with those of satellite transmission so that the socially divisive effect of cable (its comparatively low cost in high-density areas and high cost in thinly populated areas) is minimized. One of the social advantages of relatively few radio and television networks has been the sense of sharing a national experience with millions of your fellow citizens on a national occasion like a Royal Wedding or a Cup Final. This sense of community could be as easily fragmented by the new technology as the critical mass of talent needed for the production of high-quality software.

Sixth, the quality of radio and television criticism needs to match the importance of these two means of broadcasting. At present, national newspaper coverage of radio is so sparse and mean as to be almost unnoticeable, whereas television criticism in the popular press is a flattery of instinctual taste, equivalent criticism in the quality press a playing field for the liberal conscience off duty.

Seventh, the practitioners need to question their own conventions and attitudes with greater rigour. There is little awareness of the inherent romanticism of the television medium, with its built-in bias in favour of feeling at the expense of reason and the essentially dramatic nature of moving visual sequences. There is such a thing as a grammar of television, which viewers should know about. Far from letting viewers know, however, practitioners guard the secrets of their visual practices jealously, like doctors issuing illegible prescriptions—and their motives are not altogether dissimilar.

Eighth, we must not allow our enthusiasm for additional technology to hide existing defects. In particular, the sound quality of television sets is still a disgrace. Manufacturers have done little to improve that quality, partly because they say there is no particular consumer reaction, partly because improvement of sound quality might raise the price of sets. For my part, I would expect a new generation of television sets not only to give me access to further transmission channels but also to allow me to enjoy the sound of a broadcast concert on television—music being sound, first and last— rather than close-ups of performing musicians.

Ninth, since the one safe prediction in the broadcasting field is that more and more people will see feature films in their own homes, there will need to be a fair measure of co-operation between the British television and film worlds. The traditional hostility towards television of the more hidebound elements of the film industry will have to cease. And television will have to acknowledge a greater obligation towards the making of new films by a variety of transactions, be they co-production agreements, or straight payments, or the investment of seed money.

Technological plenty could spell the end of broadcasting and introduce 'narrowcasting' as the predominant means of transmission. It is my submission that except in such specialist fields as, for example, education (where 'narrowcasting' might work well), the end of broadcasting would amount to a cultural disaster. We are perfectly capable of preserving the best of our present achievement and extending that achievement with the new means at our disposal. We could, alternatively, embrace technological determinism as the new banner of free enterprise.

Come back, George Orwell, all is forgiven.

9. *Shadow Across the Screen*

RUSSELL HARTY

The first time somebody called me a television personality, I was embarrassed. That feeling later turned to annoyance. The description has about it a faint, and sometimes not so faint, air of disapproval. Certain parts of me began to suffer from numbing feelings of intellectual leprosy. As we move to the third great age of broadcasting, things are changing again, though. Some lepers are quite proud of their stumps and wave them to gawping crowds in order to attract greater attention. The gesture may be one of defiance rather than of pride.

I have been helped in the hardening of my resolve by reading, recently, the admired Anthony Powell's thoughts on the subject of the TV personality. In the fourth and last volume of his memoirs (called *The Strangers are All Gone*), he writes:

> The television personality is positively encouraged by the condition of existence to be answerable to no one but self, under no sort of restraint other than remaining a recognized 'personality'. The impression often given is that prolonged expenditure of the personality (as the Victorians used to suppose of masturbation) is cruelly hard on mind and body.

If Mr Powell is right, and he nearly is, then by the time the Third Great Age of broadcasting gets under way, I shall be nearly blind and will have great difficulty in reading the autocue. It is also a touch naïf of Mr Powell to suggest that responsibility to no one but self is both frivolous and liberating. Let us, however, assume that Mr Powell's proposition is, in general, acceptable. He has made me responsible for me. It would be foolish to pretend that I don't enjoy being me. It would be equally foolish to pretend that I do not recognize the Malvolian trap therein. The yellow stockings and

130

cross-garters are always waiting in a prop box in the wings.

A television 'personality' having been thrust upon me, allow me to explain how it came about, what benefits and what miseries it entails and what I believe or, more precisely, hope that the third age will hold.

I had always believed that power, and some wealth and a great deal of enjoyment, were enjoyed by my university ·contemporaries who were fortunate to get jobs in television. There were then—there still are now—many manifest examples of its power and influence. If you telephone Downing Street or Longleat or an oil rig in the North Sea, you are more likely to achieve some kind of interested response than if you say that you are a teacher, a taxi-driver or a traveller from Crosse and Blackwell. Indeed, if you happen, by accident, to mention Crosse and Blackwell in the course of an idle moment's television chat, you are likely to be offered a box of assorted soups. I therefore applied to the BBC, three times each year, rehearsing a list of exclusive diseases and finishing each application with a pompous statement about the particular and peculiar gifts I could offer—gifts and skills that would improve the quality of the nation's life. I sent off these dutiful applications for ten years, and nothing happened until, in a moment of fine recklessness, I appended a rude postscript to the form. The thirty-first application caught someone's eye.

I was in no way disappointed by what I found in the middle of the Second Great Age. That was 1970. Grace Wyndham Goldie and Colin Shaw had finished their task of self-reproduction, and BBC-2 was well established. At Independent Television there was an intoxicating mix of money and freedom, and it was to this liberal cocktail party that I found myself invited by Humphrey Burton, to assist in the production of the new arts programme called *Aquarius* at London Weekend.

It was not yet a time for questioning or self-doubt. Nowadays it is *de rigueur* to get up a coach party for Buxton or Gleneagles for a three-day in-depth think-in. On the agenda there are the topics of 'motivation', 'the pre-emptive configuration', 'the company's posture' and 'the audience profile'. These glorious abstracts are discussed, mainly by those who propose them, during long daily sessions. At night time people drink a lot and become indiscreet. When you get back you can remember only the nights.

There was no time for such indulgences in the *Aquarius* schedule. It was gently suggested by Mr Burton that his programme might profit from a certain vulgarity that he had detected in my approach to programme ideas. I was interested in the art of tattooing, in the desperate plight of an impoverished travelling circus, in the disaster potential of a wet Highland gathering. I found a natural director for my ideas in the massive shape of Charlie Squires, who sucked every Woodbine down to the wet root and then ground it into the floor with an unnecessary Cuban heel. His language was overripe. His approach to film-making was cavalier. For a documentary called *Derby Day* he ordered seven separate fully manned crews to cover the day itself and the activities peripheral to the race. He sat in a caravan on Epsom Downs and sent out irregular foul-mouthed commands. At seven o'clock of a warm June evening seven film cameramen came back to headquarters to tell him that they had captured fabulous shots of a toothless 80-year-old woman escaping from a bag in which she had been bound, in chains, by a wheezing husband. Seven cameramen had photographed a lost child, a Seventh Day Adventist, the popping of champagne corks, the Queen sneezing and a sheik with a wad of £20 notes placing a bet of £5,000. But not one of the seven cameramen had remembered to shoot the finish of the memorable race in which Lester Piggott rode Nijinsky to victory. An air of recriminating blue hysteria rose over the little white caravan—and yet Charlie Squires made a magical confection of the proffered material.

A year later, at a state banquet in Tokyo given to us by the Office of Culture and Tourism, which supervised our making of a documentary about life and art in Japan, Mr Squires, sitting cross-legged and forcing a little raw fish into his mouth, developed a terrible cramp, hauled his eighteen stones of flesh into a complaining arc, put out his hand to steady his bulk and disappeared through an elegantly painted but flimsy wall. As the producer of this yet unmade film, I had to paper over the cracks of this unfortunate diplomatic incident.

There are a hundred legends surrounding Squires, the man-mountain. But his chief characteristic was his hard-nosed ability to follow instinct. He did not want, and did most certainly not need, a synopsis of the film story. He wanted to be able to smell something in the air. If it was a good smell, a savoury smell, he would proceed with all convenient speed. If it was a bad smell, he would stop.

Good television operates in this way more than we care to admit. At LWT the late Cyril Bennett, my first big boss, played the instinct game. At an early meeting he asked me (told me, rather) never to propose programmes with titles like 'Whither Bulgaria?' or 'Your Children's Teeth'. Subsequently, I went to Madrid to meet Salvador Dali. I fancied that somehow, with my new-found faith in instinct, with growing confidence and with an appetite for the bizarre, we might be able to make some popular entertainment together. Dali plays dangerous games. At our first meeting he pretended to be deaf, and he made me shout my requests. The ideas that I had developed at a desk in London sounded absurd when bawled out in a moonlit courtyard in Spain. When, eventually, I had taken his measure and whispered the final moments, he smiled and anointed his fabled upturned moustaches with a separate flower of jasmin. I thought I had landed this particularly fantastic fish.

'Will your film be a considered and serious study of my art?' he asked.

'It most certainly will,' I said, and added, as a full stop of insurance, the word 'sir'.

'I don't want to do it then,' he said, and went deaf again.

At such a critical stage of any television programme's preparation you have to remember the vital teachings of Izaak Walton. If the fish has partly swallowed the bait, don't tighten your line. Let the fish swim freely and follow it up and down the stream. Observe its movements and wait until it tires. Then a twitch of the rod, your gaffe ready, and you may land it.

Dali taught me more lessons. We drove one night to the Prado, where he was to deliver a lecture. He was at that time the unofficial Court Painter to the Franco family. He had a strong desire to lecture, on an artistic subject, in Spain's most famous museum. The authorities were incensed. No living artist had ever been accorded this honour. Why should they send for this monster? Franco, however, said yes, and the iron doors swung open to admit Dali. We were driving down an avenue of limes, in Al Capone's Cadillac, a recent acquisition.

'What is the title of your lecture?' I inquired.

'*Velazquez and Me*,' he replied.

'Of course,' I murmured.

The programme was eventually made. It introduced a large number of people to the gentleman and met with some international success. It gave me an appetite for the popular, and it would not need a MORI poll to reveal the fact that Charlie and Dali and a small

133

number of other influential colleagues encouraged me to persist in that direction.

Perhaps I should be a little more modest. I had not, by the early 1970s, reached the television screen under my own name. I was concerned that those productions that I supervised should be popular. But it befell upon an autumn morning, on a cavernous waste shore in the unstilled Hebrides, that I was called to the telephone to answer a highly personal question from Cyril Bennett. LWT had lost the services of Simon Dee in distressing circumstances. They were looking for a replacement, and in those days it seemed more challenging to the programme authorities to take a chicken from their own back yard and stick it under the infra-red and see how (or if) it could perform.

An interesting shift in attitude took place when I moved from behind the camera. Whereas I had been concerned that lots of people, crowds, millions, should watch everything I had supervised and should talk about it eagerly the next morning in common rooms and in the canteens of Crosse and Blackwell, here, out in front, I wanted to hide. I suggested that the programme, a chat show, should carry a suitably anonymous name like *Opinion,* or *Confrontation* (too strong), or *Meeting-Point* (too religious). One reason for this need to hide was a fear of failure, signalled by the fact that my own name suddenly sounded grotesque. At school I was called 'Farty' until I was big enough to hit others on the nose. I presumed that the same would now apply. Bennett insisted that the programme title should be eponymous. I agreed (I had little choice) and lost weight. Bennett's unnerving philosophy was that if the programme failed, it would fail quickly, and little tarnish would stick to the name. If it were to succeed, the rewards would be.... We shall examine the rewards eventually.

The greatest help he gave me was that he allowed the programme time to settle and then time to develop. It was, for many years, a local programme, transmitted in the London area only, and then, for still unexplained reasons, bought by Grampian and RTE-2. I became well known in Camberwell and Aberdeen and remained unknown elsewhere. My home town, Blackburn, in Lancashire, never saw me, and at one municipal gathering in the Town Hall in 1975 the Mayor said to me, 'You may be a big cheese in London, but you're bugger-all in Blackburn.' When Yarwood started to do me, the studio audiences laughed loudly, but people in Kettering scratched their heads.

My belief in the need to allow a programme time to develop is absolute. So much of the machinery of television is designed to operate like an Exocet. The results must be immediate and decisive and must make a powerful hole in the opposition. The temptation to pull a programme out of the schedule if it seems nervous and wobbling is nearly irresistible. The nerve is displayed to more advantage when a controller nudges and nurtures. Bennett sent me a note after the fourth programme saying that it was the worst display of self-indulgence he had yet seen on any screen, and he presumed that things could only get better. I lost more weight and started to take *The Times Educational Supplement* again.

What the Second Great Age has proved is that the majority of viewers have welcomed the opportunity to use the set as a dating machine. He who browsed through the pages of *Radio Times,* up to 1955, would find that every week's programming was different from every other week's. No two Tuesdays were ever the same. Then, in 1955, came commercial television, with objectives other than those of education, information and entertainment. The advertisers needed to count heads. The companies had to deliver numbers—increasing numbers at that. A large audience needed to be made familiar with a landscape, a terrain with increasingly well-known landmarks and, most important, an address (Coronation Street) that you could visit regularly. The concept of a regular rendezvous is now firmly established. If it's Monday or Wednesday, it must be *Coronation Street*. If it's Tuesday or Thursday, it must be *Russell Harty*. If it's ten o'clock, it must be the News. If it's nine, it must be *Not the Nine o'Clock News*. And, since the majority of viewers are creatures of habit, the system has worked with immense success in terms of ratings.

The concern of the Third Great Age, of course, is what happens to the success of programmes like *Coronation Street, That's Life, This is Your Life?* If Age Three is to offer such fragmentation as we are promised by the proliferation of systems and hardware, will the mass audience remain faithful? Seventeen million people go to Coronation Street twice a week. The programme is a spectacular national phenomenon. It is successful in part because it is very well performed and in part because it is written with one suspicious eye on what is going on in the next street or the next stately home. There is, also, the drooping eye that ignores the fact that Pakistanis would by now have bought the corner shop and that, on the odd night in the Rover's Return, you might just catch sight of a passing homosexualist. Nevertheless, the line between fact and fiction has been triumphantly blurred, and the Sunday papers sell a great deal more copies when they explore the private lives and black eyes of the women in Mike Baldwin's factory. As yet we are safe in the certainty that a household that runs a video cassette recorder and watches *Coronation Street* would not put on a tape of the *Exorcist*, borrowed from the video library, during the transmission of the *Street*. As yet.

It is difficult, again as yet, to see how the element of surprise that has helped to establish programmes like *This is Your Life* and *Pot Black* will be affected by recording hardware. Audiences, in my experience, respond vigorously to the live event, to the surprise. I think it is hypocritical of certain commentators to say that they are not interested in the identity of Eamonn Andrews's weekly victim or in how he or she will respond to the confrontation. The programme satisfies a powerful natural curiosity. *Sunt lacrimae rerum*—and it is absurd to pretend that tears don't make good television. Mercifully, our opinions of what makes good television differ. I now opine that to make a live programme is more satisfying than to clip out little bits of boredom or untidiness.

We don't have an editing facility in the ordinary pursuance of our day's routine, and even if, occasionally, one's ears are boxed in public, then the resultant anger and shame are gradually transferred to a credit account. Grace Jones, who hit me over the head last year in a confrontation of deep personal embarrassment, landed me on the front pages of the next day's papers. The ratings, hitherto modest, began to climb. I cannot pretend that I am grateful to this demented *chanteuse*. Gratitude would be too strong a word. But I work in a marketplace, and I want people to buy things from my stall. One of the most devastating experiences of my childhood was to work on my father's fruit and vegetable pitch in Blackburn market on a Saturday afternoon. Sometimes he would snatch the card with the price of strawberries on it and replace it with a new, reduced offer. Customers would nose about, leave the neighbouring stall and form an eager queue in front of ours.

You will now have located the source of my present fear. The horrible imaginings are that in Age Three there will be a vast new Tesco of choices. Customers will be wheeling their trolleys up and down gangways of endlessly reduced offers. The store will be open at all hours. The incentives to buy will bark from tannoys at the four corners of the establishment. 'Watch Channel Eleven!', 'Spot Saturday's Deliberate Mistake and win a holiday for two in the Bahamas' (somebody from Crosse and Blackwell will win that), and 'Weren't you once hit on the head by Grace Darling?'

If you are in charge of a network, or a department, or, at the humblest level, a programme, and you are adequately relaxed about it, you do enjoy considerable benefits. The power of persuasion, a degree of wealth and popularity.

The power of persuasion means that because I like William Walton and his music, I may be able to persuade other people to taste that enjoyment. Because I enjoy listening to the exquisitely turned phrasing of Sir Harold Acton, sitting in his *quattrocento* palazzo in Florence and animadverting on Bardot and Berenson, maybe I can persuade others to share the taste. Because I enjoy the choir of St Paul's Cathedral, the extended arms of Sandy Powell and the fizzing dangers of being stranded on an oil rig in the North Sea, others will pick up a part of the message.

Degrees of wealth are relative. What wealth I accrue from my present situation, I spend in the enjoyment of the high skyline of north Yorkshire. I've never been to Annabel's. I don't wear Gucci shoes. But I can buy silence. That, at the moment, is enough.

Popularity is a sharp two-edged sword. Use it, and you can secure a corner table at the restaurant of your choice. Use it, and you can get two good seats for a sold-out theatre. Use it, and Crosse and Blackwell will pay you well to open their new plant. Use it, and they will hold the Glasgow–London train for three minutes at Preston so that you can get to wherever you're going with the minimum inconvenience. Use it, and the local butcher's shop will knock 5p off your weekend joint. Use it, and Princess Anne will ask you how you've been since last you met. But the other edge can be a destructive instrument. Construction workers hang over building sites and make remarks about your manhood. Small crowds discuss your identity, within your hearing: 'Can't remember his name but he's the one your mother doesn't like.' Girls at the check-out counter at Marks and Spencer pick out your purchases and mouth at each other, 'Fancy *him* buying food.' And, at its lowest and most depressing ebb, if there does happen to be a proposition of a physical nature and a subsequent struggle under the duvet, your new-found friend, disregarding the urgent proportions

137

of your body, usually says, 'What's Elton John really like?'

So, having wandered this far, like a fawn in a thicket, I find myself up against that barbed-wire fence that marks the boundary of the Third Great Age of television. I could attempt to o'erleap it. Circumstances will probably drive me that way in any case.

If I were a very clever fawn, which I am not, I might with minimum crural inconvenience, attempt to straddle it. Over there the grass is rich, high, lush (or so it says in the brochures). No self-respecting animal would absolutely starve. But it might get lost. Over there is a little like America. Over there. The law of that moneyed jungle is the law of the scrap heap. The shores of television are littered with pilots—one-off wrecks—venturers into the unknown, who set off with money, machination, management and only one try.

In my own age, in my own pastureland, I have been a protected species. I have been rationed. The audience has been rationed. I have never been in the envious position of being a Woganesque black-market commodity, but word has got around, and the commodity called 'Harty' has been asked for, and sampled, at various counters.

The store manager of BBC-2 hasn't yet put me an offer at 8.10 on a Monday night—opposite a *Panorama* on 'Whither Bulgaria?' or a *World in Action* on 'Your Children's Teeth'. Protected species maybe, but not so much in danger of extinction that one is placed in an OK corral. Manoeuvring, on the scale permitted by Age 2, brought the most surprising programmes to satisfyingly large numbers. *Not the Nine o'Clock News* may have been a great triumph in its final iconoclastic spasms, but it started small. In the beginning the canteen at Crosse and Blackwell barely responded to the idea of three boys and a bright girl bouncing on a trampoline of innuendo and shouting 'Knickers' at the people. In America they would have been dismissed after the first bounce. Here they were allowed to jump higher and higher.

But over this theoretical fence, where many more energetic animals are going to display themselves for attention, surely those who pay to watch the wild life will be distracted? Shall all the glue of popular television *(Coronation Street, This is Your Life, Pot Black)*— and then all the imitators and opponents—be spread so thinly that nothing holds? Television, thereby, would perhaps become socially less important—and who shall say that that would be a bad thing? But it also may becomes less fun for those who are involved, and who shall say that that would be a good thing?

During what is left of my particular journey I want to present an appetizing variety of attractive wares on my stall, sometimes to appear in the morning papers. I want to earn enough to savour this morning's prospect of a high wisp of mist over the hills. So I'll go over the fence. Of course I shall. But I suspect—polite form of 'I fear'—that much of what I have so energetically presented on Tuesdays and Thursdays will go unremarked in the Crosse and Blackwell canteen on Wednesdays and Fridays.

'Did you see Steve Davis hit a billiard ball out of Harty's mouth last night?' she asks, as she slaps a label on the mixed veg.

'No.'

'Did you record it?'

'No. I watched the Royal Wedding.'

'Again?'

'Yes, again. Him? *He* was polishing his video disc.'